BUFFALO
BUSINESS PIONEERS

BUFFALO
BUSINESS PIONEERS

• INNOVATION IN THE NICKEL CITY •

NANCY BLUMENSTALK MINGUS

THE
History
PRESS

Published by The History Press
Charleston, SC
www.historypress.com

First published 2021

Manufactured in the United States

ISBN 9781467146685

Library of Congress Control Number: 2020945753

To my former colleagues and students at SUNY Empire State College.

CONTENTS

PREFACE

This book had its start in a college course I developed for Empire State College in 2013. I was teaching in a special residency–based business management program, and we were looking for a general education history course that the business students would be more interested in than a generic history course. It became a popular option with the students, and it taught them the basics of business as well as the history of innovation in Buffalo and the rest of the country.

My interest in inventors and innovation, however, dates back much further. My father, Louis Blumenstalk, was an inventor—although he didn't think of himself as one. He was designing solar houses on rotating foundations in the mid-1960s. Although he was not quite like Rick Moranis's character in *Honey, I Shrunk the Kids*, he was constantly tinkering with devices that would make things easier for us. In 1972, the telephone company he worked for installed the second "all electronic" (i.e., computerized) telephone company switching system in the country. The first in the world was installed at Disney World in 1970. My father's installation was driven primarily by eight printed circuit board switches that cost around $1,000 each, and they failed regularly. Rather than continue to buy totally new boards, my father decided to build a device that showed him where the failure was. Using LEDs to indicate where there was or wasn't current, he could plug in any board—not just the switch boards—to test. He named the machine D.E.B.E (pronounced like "Debbie"), which stood for "Does Everything But Eat." When we tried to get him to patent it, he said, "Oh, anyone can build one of these." He didn't think he had created anything special, and we eventually stopped bugging him.

When he passed away in 1992, in my father's World War II paperwork, we discovered that he had been given a medal for inventing an improved sight for the M-1 rifle that the army then used in production. Had we known that, we would have pressed harder. A patent for a device similar to D.E.B.E was applied for in 1974, and it was granted in 1976 to a German inventor. D.E.B.E. predated that.

Unfortunately, my father was not the only one to think his inventions were nothing special. Many creative people dismiss their ideas as something anyone could come up with. The people profiled in this book knew better. They recognized the significance of their ideas and turned them into important contributions to humanity. I hope you enjoy their stories.

ACKNOWLEDGEMENTS

Several people helped create this book, and I am grateful to them all. Most notable is my daughter, Paige Donatelli, who provided copyediting, image enhancement and general moral support. My sister, Jan McDonald; my sister-in-law, Judy Kaufman; and super librarian Cynthia VanNess helped immensely with the research. Thanks, too, to all the people who allowed me to use images from their collections. They are acknowledged individually in the image captions. Lastly, I want to thank my editor, Banks Smither, for his patience, as the COVID-19 virus caused numerous deadline slippages. Despite all that, we did it together!

INTRODUCTION

W hen most people think of Buffalo, New York, they think of mounds of snow, its football team's four consecutive failed Super Bowl appearances and Buffalo wings. But well before the birth of the city's most well-known invention, Buffalo was a hotbed of innovation. At its peak, the city was the eighth-largest in the United States, and still today, it is the second-largest metropolitan area in New York State.

In fact, the world today would be quite a different place without Buffalo-area inventions. This section introduces readers to the history of the city, its unique collection of businesses based on inventions and firsts and how those businesses and inventions changed the world.

Buffalo, New York, is located at the eastern end of Lake Erie in western New York, approximately three hundred miles due west of New York's capital city, Albany, and four hundred miles northwest of New York City. Founded at the mouth of Buffalo Creek, now known as the Buffalo River, the city is in a prime strategic trading location, which led to the settlement of the area by Europeans in the late 1700s. How the city was named is a matter that is up for debate, but it is most likely that the city took its name from the creek on which it grew; and that creek was most likely named after a Native American the locals called Buffalo because of his resemblance to the animal.

Buffalo can credit much of its growth to the individuals profiled in this book, but the innovators who were selected are just some of the area's best. There are dozens more who could also qualify as Buffalo business pioneers. Perhaps they can be discussed in a follow-up volume. The inventors and inventions that are included in this book are covered as close to a chronological sequence as possible to help the reader understand the context of the city and the nation when the inventors created their products and how they aided in the progression of future inventions.

We will start in 1842 with Joseph Dart, whose grain elevator allowed the city to become a transportation hub, which it continued to be until its 1950s high point. Next, we will move on to Birdsill Holly, whose many inventions in fire systems and heating helped keep everyone safer and warmer. Maria Love opened the first crèche (i.e., daycare) in the country in 1881, allowing women to work away from home if they needed or wanted to. Alfred Southwick's creation of the electric chair is not regarded today as one of the more socially acceptable inventions, but as you'll see, at the time, it was considered not only acceptable but also humane. Louise Bethune was the first professional female architect in the country, and she set a positive example for all women entering traditionally male professions after her. Willis Carrier, who invented modern air conditioning in 1902, is clearly the heaviest hitter of the group, as he changed not only where people could comfortably live in the United States but where they could live around the world. Despite popular local legend, Buffalo businessman John Oishei did not invent windshield wipers, but, as other innovators have done over the years, he did build on other people's inventions to become the dominant provider of them for decades. Most people have never heard of Glenn Curtiss, but he—not the Wright brothers—was the most creative aviator of his time. Not only did he invent improvements to airplanes well into the 1920s, but he also designed early versions of air boats and travel trailers. Most people have not heard of Alex Osborn, either, but anyone who has ever been in a problem-solving meeting has used his invention: brainstorming. Robert Rich Sr.'s non-dairy whipped topping doesn't sound like an earthshaking invention, but Rich's use of soybeans proved that they were viable alternatives to dairy, and it started the entire frozen non-dairy products industry. Wilson Greatbatch's innovation was accidental, as were Oishei's and Rich's, and his implantable pacemaker has saved millions of lives. Our last innovators, Frank and Teressa Bellissimo—more than a century after Dart—turned a chicken waste product into the most popular appetizer and snack in the United States, if not the world.

What follows are the stories of these creative individuals and the businesses they developed. These are not intended to be thorough biographies; however, each of these profiles does include one or more facts that are not normally found in brief biographical pieces nor easily found in nonbiographical pieces. Hopefully, they wet readers' interests to pursue the more detailed biographies that are available on most of these people.

1.

JOSEPH DART AND THE GRAIN ELEVATOR

The first widely regarded inventor in Buffalo was Joseph Dart, who, in 1842, constructed a new way to load and unload grain that revolutionized the shipping industry. By 1855, Buffalo was the largest grain port in the world, and the total amount of goods shipped through the city was valued at nearly $50 million at a time when average wages were $52 per year. This chapter reviews the early settlement of the area, the need for Dart's innovation, how it worked and why it was critical to shipping not just in Buffalo but around the world.

Buffalo had grown from a scattered eighteenth-century settlement base to a town of about 1,500 residents by 1810. As its reputation for being a good place for business grew, so did its population, reaching more than 2,000 in 1820. The opening of the Erie Canal in 1825 brought a flood of new residents, and by 1830, the population had more than quadrupled in size. Improved transportation, better livelihoods and a developing infrastructure also drove the city's growth. When the city incorporated in 1832, it already had six churches, a theater, ten general stores, six hotels and two financial institutions. The population's children attended one of the ten schools that were already operating, and there was a public library to support their studies. The students' parents and travelers could enjoy the products of the several breweries that were already established. In addition to working at the businesses mentioned above, residents were employed in shoe factories, tanneries and the budding smelting and forge industry. Not only could many amenities be found in the bourgeoning city, but the surrounding agricultural area supported residents with a rich variety of fresh vegetables and grain, especially wheat, which some estimates say gave the area an export income in excess of $6 million. The ability to use and transport both the manufactured goods and agricultural products turned Buffalo into an important trading port.

Another component that encouraged the growth of Buffalo as a trading port was the development of the Buffalo Harbor. Well into the 1800s, the fastest and easiest way to travel in the world was via the waterways, but Buffalo Creek was often unnavigable even for vessels as small as canoes because of a persistent sand bar that formed at its mouth. So, in 1823, villagers, led by Samuel Wilkeson, decided to fix the problem by moving the mouth of the creek some one thousand feet to the south. The installation of two new piers to keep the sand bar at bay also provided better harbor space, which was instrumental in Buffalo's ability to secure the coveted western terminus designation on the Erie Canal.

Prior to the opening of the canal, eastbound grain traffic from the Midwest plains used boats traveling on a variety of rivers to the Mississippi and on to New Orleans. Once in New Orleans, the grain continued east via early, rough, underdeveloped and often mountainous roads or on boats that navigated around Florida and then north. All of this tedious transportation added up, leading to a grain cost of about one hundred dollars a ton. The canal allowed grain as well as other commodities to be shipped across the Great Lakes to Buffalo, then east to Albany and south to New York City, where it could either be used or continue on to other national and international ports. The previous three- to six-week journey was shortened to just eight or nine days. The canal saved not only time, but it allowed for an impressive cost reduction to about six to ten dollars per ton, which was less than one-tenth its previous cost.

By 1841, the city population had doubled again to more than eighteen thousand, and with the harbor improvements in place, the port was processing close to two million tons of grain. But it was a tedious process that required the bags of grain to be unloaded from a ship, sorted, transported and then loaded into a storage facility, where it waited to be loaded onto another vessel. The chain of work was called transhipment, and it was necessary because the size of the canal boats was significantly smaller than the arriving lake schooners. Only barges specifically designed to fit in the forty-foot-wide-by-four-feet-deep canal could navigate it, especially the locks, which were only twenty feet wide. Transhipment took many men making hundreds of trips per day, and they were still only able to move about two thousand bushels a day. On top of this, on windy, rainy days, which occurred about 25 percent of the time, nothing could be moved at all.

Watching these events unfold led Joseph Dart to realize that the city needed a dramatically improved way to load and unload grain. He envisioned harnessing the power of steam to streamline operations, which he hoped would revolutionize not only Buffalo's port operations but the entire shipping industry—and that it did. As Dart himself noted in an 1865 speech at the Buffalo Historical Society, his invention had "a bearing on not only the citizens of this community but also upon an immensely larger number of people, whose grain productions are sent and whose bread supplies are received through our hands." While this may sound pompous, it was true.

Joseph Dart was born on April 30, 1799, in Middle Haddam, Connecticut. His parents were Joseph and Sarah Dart, and he was their third son. He started his business career as an apprentice in a hat factory outside Danbury Connecticut, about sixty miles from his home. According to some sources, he moved west, in 1819, to Utica, New York, where he worked for two years, and then he moved to Buffalo in 1821. His first known business venture in Buffalo was also apparel-related. He partnered in 1822 in a hat, cap, leather and fur store located at the southeast corner of Main and Swan Streets with a man whose name, ironically, was Joseph Stocking. Dart was an astute businessman, recognizing that communication was key to sales. Because there were many Native American traders in the area at that time, Dart learned the various local dialects of the members of the Six Nations (also known as the Iroquois Confederacy), which consisted of the Cayuga, Mohawk, Oneida, Onondaga, Seneca and Tuscarora tribes. A popular story regularly recounted in biographical notes on Dart is that whenever Native Americans came to town, they stopped at Dart's shop and would often place their valuables in his care throughout their visit.

Joseph Dart had been in Buffalo for nearly a decade when he married Dotha Dennison in 1830. She was born on July 31, 1809, in Norfolk, Connecticut, about sixty miles from Dart's hometown of Middle Haddam, but it is unknown where and when they actually met. The couple lived in a number of different places over the years before finally moving to the old Baldwin stone house at the northeast corner of Georgia and Niagara Streets in 1853. They had seven children, but several died young.

Records indicate that Dart remained a hat and fur merchant until 1837, which was also when a great economic "panic" hit America. From 1837 to 1843, the U.S. economy was in a deep recession; banks failed, and unemployment went as high as 25 percent. At the time, the Panic of

Joseph Dart portrait. *From the collection of the Buffalo History Museum, general photograph collection, Persons–D.*

1837 was the worst financial downturn in the country's history, and it appears that Dart's business failed as part of this. After his store failed, he began to focus on the grain trade passing through Buffalo Harbor.

At the time, Dart considered three people to be the greatest inventors in the fields of transportation, clothing and food. These inventors were Robert Fulton, who developed the steam engine for faster transportation; Eli Whitney, whose cotton gin revolutionized the clothing industry; and Oliver Evans, who invented a faster way to mill flour. And it was the combination of the work of two of these inventors on which Dart built his grain elevator: a steam-powered elevator that used buckets similar to those Evans had in his mill.

Oliver Evans was born in Newport, Delaware, in 1755, and he and his brothers co-owned the Red Clay Creek Mill, which, despite its name, was a flour mill. In 1785, he helped automate the mill, and with his design, he cut the manual labor down to 20 percent of the previous work. He tried to convince other mills to use his design, but they were reluctant to do so. When the U.S. Patent office opened in 1790, Evans applied for a patent on his technology, and he received patent number three. He continued to invent things, such as an amphibious vehicle, a steam-powered wagon and early attempts at refrigeration.

From Dart's 1865 speech before the Buffalo Historical Society, we know that Dart was familiar with Evans's inventions. The speech also gives us insight into Dart's thought processes before, during and after his invention. It was his observations of the slowness of the transhipment process and the delays caused by poor weather that led him on his journey into the grain trade. As he noted, "The harbor was often crowded with vessels, waiting for a change of weather. In these circumstances, I determined, in 1841, to try steam power in the transfer of grain for commercial purposes."

Despite the fact that many people thought Dart was crazy to attempt such a device, he was convinced he "could built [*sic*] a warehouse of large capacity for storage, with an adjustable elevator and conveyors, to be worked by steam; and so arranged as to transfer grain from vessels to boats or bins, with cheapness and dispatch." Although it took him a year to bring the plan to fruition, he was ultimately successful. And once the idea was proven to work, the elevators spread throughout Buffalo and the world. Dart said, "Indeed, the building I erected may perhaps be called the parent...of all others; for I believe it was the first steam transfer and storage elevator in the world."

Because Dart's background was primarily in retail businesses, Dart turned to engineer Robert Dunbar for the design and construction of the elevator. Dunbar was born December 13, 1812, in Carnbee Fifeshire, Scotland, and moved to Buffalo in 1834. It was Dunbar's practical engineering skills that turned the dream into reality. As was noted in Dunbar's obituary in 1890, the steam grain elevator was responsible for the "commercial prosperity of the city, for it would be difficult to conceive of Buffalo without its grain elevators, and of the present system Mr. Dunbar was the father." Although Dunbar took credit for the entire elevator "invention," it is hard to say how much of the design came from each of the two men.

Dart and Dunbar selected what was then the foot of Commercial Street on the Evans Ship Canal, one of a series of canals that connected the Erie Canal to Buffalo Creek and Lake Erie, as a location for their first elevator. This is the area near today's *Vietnam Veteran's Monument*. There is a commemorative plaque marking the location.

Unlike modern grain elevators, which are constructed of concrete, Dart's first elevator was constructed from wood. The original elevator was seven stories tall and contained three main sections. The primary working component was referred to as the "marine leg," which transported the grain in buckets from a ship to the storage areas that were generally called "the house." Prior to being stored, the grain passed through a weighing hopper, which both weighed and cleaned the grain. Once the grain was in the elevator, it was stored in the house until an outgoing ship was ready to take it on the next stage of its journey. On the top of the elevator was a cupola that the marine leg could tuck up into when it was not in use. After a ship entered the unloading slip, the leg was lowered down into the ship's cargo hold. Dart's original elevator had a top, yet some of the later ones did not, which often made the work for the laborers more dangerous, and it also made it easier for fires to spread.

The first ship to be unloaded with the new elevator was the schooner *Philadelphia*, which held 4,515 bushels of wheat. That original elevator stored 55,000 bushels of grain, which were loaded by a conveyor belt with two-

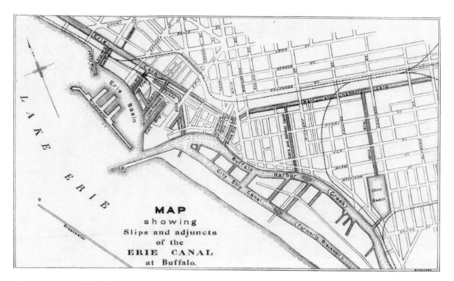

Map of the Buffalo Harbor showing the canals. *Courtesy of Whitford, 1906.*

Buffalo Harbor showing Dart Elevator. *Courtesy of the* Buffalo Courier, *December 9, 1917.*

quart buckets spaced twenty-eight inches apart. The buckets could move at approximately six miles per hour, which meant that the elevator could unload 1,000 bushels (32,000 quarts) an hour, half of the daily capacity of manual unloading.

Dart and Dunbar continued to tweak the design in terms of both loading and unloading speed and storage capacity. Decreasing the distance between the buckets improved the speed of the elevator. The buckets were moved from the original twenty-eight-inch spacing to twenty-two inches and later to sixteen inches, which also effectively doubled the elevator speed to about two thousand bushels an hour. Further improvements switched the buckets from two quarts to eight quarts, which were merely twelve inches apart, nearly quadrupling the speed again, all the way to between six thousand and seven thousand bushels an hour. In comparison to the original manual labor rate, this latter elevator did nearly four days' worth of work an hour.

In 1845, the holding capacity of the original elevator was doubled to 110,000 bushels. Once it could hold more grain, Dart added a second leg to the elevator, which made it capable of unloading two ships at a time; one on the Evans Ship Canal and the other one on Buffalo Creek, now known as the Buffalo River. Dart's idea gained traction, and by 1860, there were ten elevators in the harbor that could store a total of 1.5 million bushels of grain. It is estimated that by the 1860s, 40 to 70 million bushels of grain passed through Buffalo.

Although several grain elevators still stand in Buffalo Harbor, the Dart elevator does not. Dart sold the original elevator to David S. Bennett in 1853, and in 1863, it succumbed to fire. Its reincarnation was named the Bennett Elevator, which alone could store six hundred thousand bushels of grain. By that time, there were twenty-seven elevators in town, many of which had also been designed by Robert Dunbar. By 1899, there were forty grain elevators, some more than 250 feet tall, looming over the harbor. These elevators could not only load and unload ships, but many also had chutes that could direct grain to neighboring elevators or to a nearby mill.

Despite the fact that the number of manual laborers for the actual transhipment process was decreased significantly, there was still a measure of manual work required. New tradesmen dubbed "scoopers" evolved, and these workers made sure that the grain in the ships was actually reaching the buckets. They were especially needed when the ships were close to empty, as they had to scrape the grain from the edges of the ship's hold into the elevator buckets. The scoopers worked in teams of twenty-six, and they were supervised by a "scooper boss," who often needed to act

Bennett Elevator, Buffalo Harbor.
Courtesy of the Library of Congress.

as a referee in fights on and off the docks. Scoopers received $1.85 per one thousand bushels, loaded and unloaded. What is most interesting about this job is that, although the initial manual labor decreased as more elevators were constructed, the number of workers ultimately increased with the grain elevators. Prior to the elevator, there were about five hundred men working as grain handlers, but in the heydays of the elevators, there were around two thousand scoopers.

The increase in grain transhipment capabilities in the harbor caused a demand for ships as well, and by 1857, thirty lake steamers had been constructed in the Buffalo shipyard and others in Black Rock. And the shorter travel times meant that there was a steady stream of travelers who were primarily heading west. More than one hundred thousand people traveled through Buffalo from the 1830s to the 1850s. Some people even stayed in town, adding to the population growth, which wasn't always a positive thing. The Canal Street area of the city became notorious for violent drunken behavior due to its nearly one hundred saloons, dance halls and bordellos, which were patronized by visitors and locals.

Like many true innovators, Dart liked to start new businesses and other ventures. After his success in the grain industry, Dart moved on to the lumber industry, building and operating a lumber yard with a planing mill. The business was originally called Dart Brothers because it was owned by Dart, his brother and his brother-in-law, but when Dart's brother-in-law left the company, the remaining pair changed the name to Dart and Brother. Joseph Dart was also one of the founders of the Buffalo Historical Society and one of Buffalo's preeminent private schools, the Buffalo Female Academy.

Dart died on September 28, 1879, in his stone home on the corner of Niagara and Georgia Streets, and his funeral was also held there. In an 1885 issue of *Harper's Magazine*, a profile of Buffalo included a discussion of the effects his elevator had had on the city.

Dart is criticized regularly for his failure to appropriately acknowledge all of the individuals who helped him realize his dream, but, as Dart noted in his speech to the Buffalo Historical Society, virtually all inventions are improvements on those that already exist—both on paper and in reality.

NORTHEAST CORNER OF NIAGARA AND GEORGIA STREETS.

Above: Buffalo Harbor. *Courtesy of* Harper's Magazine, *June 1885.*

Left: Dart's House. *Courtesy of the* Buffalo Times, *May 23, 1909.*

> *In noticing this new use of the elevator, it is worthy of remark, that some of the most useful inventions have not been discoveries of new principles or methods of mechanical action, but new applications of methods and principles already known.*

Dart was referring to the fact that Evans's elevator and Fulton's steam engine fell into this category of invention; yet the same is true for his and many of the other innovators' inventions profiled in this book.

In this same speech, Dart clearly credited Evans for providing a background idea. It took up nearly 25 percent of the talk and the entire conclusion:

JOSEPH DART

Joseph Dart in his later years. *Courtesy of the* Buffalo Courier, *December 9, 1917.*

Oliver Evans had a religious idea, that he was raised up by Providence to confer important benefits on his fellow men; and, certainly, could he now be aware how extensively his improvements are used, how wonderfully, by their means, trade has been extended, commerce increased, food cheapened, and the general welfare of mankind advanced, he would be satisfied that his laborious and perplexing life had not been in vain.

So, Dart acknowledged Evans; although, admittedly, he hardly mentioned Dunbar's contributions. But what Dart did was not just envision a steam-powered elevator; he also funded its construction and turned it into a highly profitable business. And that business, in turn, helped make Buffalo one of the largest grain processing centers in the world.

2.

BIRDSILL HOLLY AND THE FIRE HYDRANT

Birdsill Holly was a prolific inventor. In 1869, he refined the fire hydrant and water supply system that numerous large cities later implemented. Unfortunately, Chicago chose not to and shortly afterward had its massive conflagration. This chapter describes Holly's hydrant system invention as well as several of his other inventions and the businesses that he developed to support his inventions.

Birdsill Holly Jr. was born near Auburn, New York, a picturesque village at the north end of Owasco Lake, one of the Finger Lakes, on November 8, 1820. (Note that other spellings of Holly's first name include Birdsall, Birdsel and Birdzel, and his last name is sometimes spelled Holley or Hawley.) It is likely that his family was living near the town at the time because his father was a mechanic and millwright working as part of the construction crew that was drawn there to build the then new Auburn Prison. After the completion of the prison, Holly Sr. and many of his previous coworkers were hired to build a new Presbyterian seminary, also in Auburn.

As work on the Seminary was nearing completion, the new Auburn Prison started a job training program that drove many of the town's technical tradespeople out of business; this included Holly Sr. For a brief time in 1821, he tried his hand at farming, and later that same year, he purchased property in Seneca Falls, New York, about sixteen miles west of Auburn at the top of Cayuga Lake, the largest of New York's Finger Lakes. When the family moved to Seneca Falls, New York, Holly Sr. worked again as a mechanic and millwright.

Unfortunately, Holly Sr. died in 1828 at only thirty-seven years old, forcing Holly Jr. to look for a job. As a mere lad, at ten years old, Holly Jr. became the apprentice of a local cabinetmaker. Although the specific cabinetmaker is not known, speculation is that it was Prentiss Field, who specialized in chairs, as eleven years later, Holly married Field's daughter Elizabeth.

Not happy with cabinetmaking, Holly moved on to an apprenticeship in a machinist's shop, but the record is unclear as to where or with whom he did this apprenticeship. If it was in Seneca Falls, it is likely that it was with George McClary, who owned the only machine shop in town at the time. When Holly was

Birdsill Holly. *Courtesy of District Heating, 1915.*

still in his late teens, he took a job as the superintendent of a machine shop in Uniontown, Pennsylvania, and later, he opened a machine shop of his own, presumably in the same town, where he manufactured mill parts, pumps and water wheels.

In his early twenties, Holly moved back to Seneca Falls, where he ultimately started a new machining company named Silsby, Race and Holly. Horace Silsby, the first named partner in the firm, had arrived in Seneca Falls in 1836 and had run a series of companies manufacturing axes, stove regulators and pumps. Just a few years older than Holly, Silsby was born in Sheffield, Connecticut, in 1817. Through his manufacturing companies, Silsby became one of the leading citizens of Seneca Falls, and he died there in August 1905.

Holly apparently worked in one of these Silsby companies before being brought in as a partner in the new venture in 1848, the same year the first Women's Rights Convention was held in Seneca Falls. Holly's new company produced steam-powered fire engines and hydraulic components. Although Silsby's obituary states that Holly didn't join the firm until 1853, other documents state that he joined in 1848. Because of the company's location on an island in the Seneca River, the company was sometimes referred to as "The Island Works" and ultimately covered five acres.

It was in 1849, while Holly was a partner at Silsby, Race and Holly, that he received his first patent, which was, like most of his patents, water related.

Perhaps inspired by the falls themselves or by his childhood around the water of the Finger Lakes, Holly's first patent was for a water pump. As noted with Joseph Dart in the previous chapter, the 1840s and 1850s were decades of explosive growth in the steam power industry, so it is not surprising that Holly's next major patent, a steam-powered engine pump created in 1855, moved him toward steam as well. Along with his partner, Silsby, Holly saw that this pump would be a boon to the fire-fighting world, and together, they created the Silsby fire engine, first produced in 1856. It quickly turned into a bestseller, with more than one thousand sold, making the company the largest fire engine manufacturer in the world.

The Silsby fire engine used two of Holly's inventions, the rotary steam-cylinder engine and the aforementioned pump. The initial fire engine weighed nearly five tons and could produce sixty pounds of water pressure and, even when connected to six different hoses, was capable of creating a waterspout of nearly two hundred feet with each. Other engines at the time used a different pressure system and could not pump as far as the Sibsy did. Several Silsby engines have survived over the years, and they have developed an almost cult-like following from avid fire history afficionados.

Holly left the Seneca Falls business and moved to Lockport, New York, in 1859. Receiving financial support from Washington Hunt and Thomas Flagler, Holly formed the Holly Manufacturing Company, which made fire hydrants, fire engines, rotary pumps and cistern pumps, as well as sewing machines, flat irons, fabric fluters and skeins. The building was located on Lock Street on the edge of the canal and was originally five stories tall

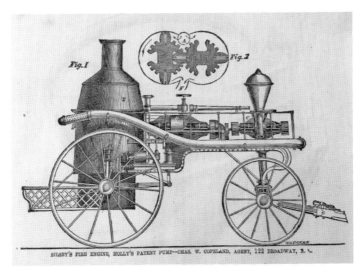

SILSBY'S FIRE ENGINE, HOLLY'S PATENT PUMP—CHAS. W. COPELAND, AGENT, 122 BROADWAY, N. Y.

Silsby engine. *From the author's collection.*

Holly Manufacturing's number 9 flat iron. *From the author's collection.*

with a foundry and boiler manufacturing building nearby. At its peak, the facility employed more than five hundred people.

As is common with most inventors, Holly continued to develop new water-related innovations. Four years after Holly established himself in Lockport, he created what most historians consider his greatest invention: the Holly system for fire protection and water works. The system was first used in 1863, in Holly's hometown of Lockport. This system was based on his rotary pumps and was originally powered by a water wheel; later, they were powered by steam engines, which brought water to hydrants in the business center of the city. What was unique about the system at this time was that it did not use a water reservoir to supply the water and water pressure. This made it more powerful and easier to maintain.

It is important to remember that, in 1863, there were only thirty-three states, and they were embroiled in a Civil War. President Lincoln had just abolished slavery. The southern states were still largely rural, while the northern states were becoming heavy industrial centers. Buffalo had grown to be the tenth-largest city in the country, and most of the urban buildings throughout the nation were made of wood. Fire was a constant threat to businesses and homes, and although Holly's earlier fire engine invention helped, people still kept their water buckets full in case a fire broke out, and large fires were combated by "bucket brigades," which passed full leather water buckets toward a fire and the empty buckets back to a water source. This inherent time delay in extinguishing fires allowed them to spread quickly.

At that time, it was also the case that very few municipalities had fire companies, and where there were organized fire companies, they were still largely volunteer-based. The firemen's gear was heavy and bulky, and they had to pump water from the "engines" for it to reach the flames. With Holly's system, hydrants were already in place, and the water was available without manual pumping. In 1869, Holly improved the hydrant in a second patent, bringing international attention to the system, which was ultimately adopted in more than two thousand municipalities in the United States and

New pumping engine and automatic pressure regulator for the Holly system of water supply and fire protection. *From the author's collection.*

Canada. Not only did it set the standard for fire systems but for the general water distribution systems that are still in place today.

The newspapers of the late 1860s and early 1870s were full of reports from citizen committees that were visiting Holly installations to consider them for their own towns. From relatively rural areas, such as Lockport itself, to large metropolises, including Cincinnati, there were glowing reports of the functioning of the systems. The following is a quote from a Covington, Kentucky report that was printed in the *Cincinnati Enquirer* on October 16, 1869.

> *We find the officers and citizens of all the cities having the Holly system in operation, are, without a single exception, fully satisfied with, and even enthusiastic on, the entire success and efficiency of their systems, and unanimous in the conviction that it accomplishes all, and even more than was promised or expected. If our counsel and citizens could see the white, sparkling and transparent waters at Binghamton, gushing from their numerous fountains, flowing from countless faucets, or thrown with startling force through ten different firehoses at the same time, we think they would*

concur with us that the system is as far superior to the old reservoir plan with its impure supply and sluggish flow as the railroad system of travel is superior to the old canal or stagecoach lines of locomotion.

The same article includes the committee's recommendation:

In conclusion, we would add that the machinery made by the Holly Manufacturing Company is superior in beauty, finish, adaption and ingenious combinations to anything in that line we have ever examined; and the company were shipping the machinery for two distinct works in the state of Michigan, and have in process of construction works for Dayton and Columbus, besides many other contracts yet to be filled. We are assured by the company that if we bargain with them for our machinery, that they will make it the most powerful, elegant and complete of anything they have erected, for the reason that it will be an extensive advertisement of their works, being the first southern city, in close proximity to the city of Cincinnati, and on the great lines of travel east and west, as well as north and south.

Despite these glowing reviews, Holly also personally went on the road to meet with a variety of municipal officials. One of the cities to which Holly traveled was Chicago, yet he was unsuccessful in his bid to sell his fire system there. There is evidence that the Chicago Public Works officials recommended purchasing the system as early as 1868—and again in 1870—but the city did not do so. Within a year, the Great Chicago Fire of 1871 would burn down around seventeen thousand buildings, killing three hundred people and leaving one hundred thousand homeless. It was estimated that this single fire caused $200 million in damages, which is the equivalent to $4.2 billion today.

Holly's company continued to be successful, and many of his family members came into the business to work with him. But he started to lose local support when he divorced his first wife, Elizabeth, and remarried a much younger woman who had once been his ward. Holly and his new wife, Sophia, built a large family home at 31 Chestnut Street in Lockport.

Although he is primarily remembered for his fire-related inventions, Holly's greatest contribution may have actually been his introduction of what he referred to as district heating. Seeing that the water system portion of the business was going well, by 1876, Holly had turned his sights toward ways to more effectively use steam power to heat homes and other buildings. To test his theories, Holly ran a wooden pipe underground between his Chestnut Street home and his barn, which proved the concept would work. Building on that success, he extended a one-hundred-foot pipe to a neighbor's house, and with that, he was able to heat his neighbor's home.

In 1877, Holly merged the Holly Manufacturing Company with a new venture to form the Holly Steam Combination Company. The new company developed a commercial application of his notion of district heating. This started with a large boiler located at the plant, which provided the steam to several Lockport buildings via a continuous loop circuit of water pipes. This loop sent out the steam and returned condensed water. Even in this early era, the pipes were insulated to minimize the heat loss between buildings in the loop. New York City purchased one of the largest systems sold, and even today, much of the heat in that city is provided via steam. Building owners were charged by how much steam they used, which was measured by water meters. The heat was supplied to the buildings via specially designed radiators that ranged from simple affairs to ornate furniture-like ensembles.

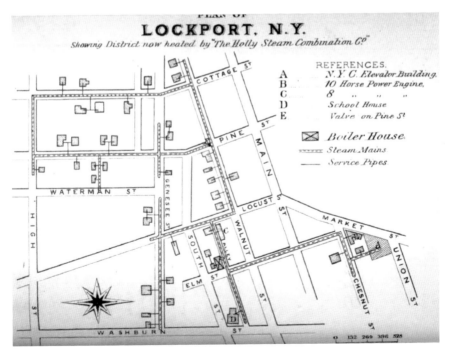

Lockport map showing heating connections. *Courtesy of the* Holly Pamphlet, *1878.*

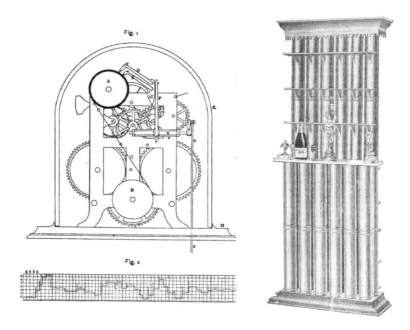

Left: Heat meter designed by Holly. *Right*: A lavishly styled radiator option designed by Holly. *Courtesy of the* Holly Pamphlet, *1878.*

Although he was primarily known for the inventions previously noted, Holly had more than 150 patents. The following is a partial list of Holly patents in ascending order:

June 5, 1849	Pumps	6500
July 25, 1854	Mortising Machine	11403
February 6, 1855	Rotary Pump	12350
July 3, 1855	Turbine Wheels	13172
July 13, 1858	Stoves, Furnaces	20919
May 8, 1860	Sewing Machines	28176
July 14, 1863	Pumps, Improvements	39259
November 15, 1863	Pumps, Improvements	45040
January 31, 1865	Hot Air Furnace	46107
September 14, 1869	Hydrants, Improvements	94749
November 5, 1872	Water-Supply for Cities, Improvements	RE5133 E
October 5, 1880	Steam Heating Radiator	232821
May 10, 1881	Steam Meters	241217
August 15, 1882	Tunnel for Street Mains	262670
May 14, 1889	Vise	403107

GENERAL VIEW OF THE WORKS OF THE HOLLY MANUFACTURING CO.

Holly Manufacturing Company aerial view. *Courtesy of the* Manufacturer and Builder, *1888.*

Birdsill Holly died on April 27, 1894, but he had not been active in the company for many years prior to that time. He had left the company in the hands of Harvey Gaskill, an important inventor in his own right, but when Gaskill died suddenly in 1889, Holly's son Frank took charge. Holly's second wife, Sophia, died in 1900 at the age of only fifty-four, and his first wife, Elizabeth, outlived them all, dying at age eighty-six in 1909.

Even with his more than 150 patents, perhaps Holly's most intriguing invention, a towering overlook to view Niagara Falls, never saw fruition. He recognized that Niagara Falls could be one of the world's largest tourist attractions and proposed the construction of a 700-foot-tall nineteen-story observation building. A 300-foot tower had been built, but it had been demolished in the 1870s, and Holly lobbied heavily for a new, taller one. He was unable to garner investors in the construction, however, so it only ever remained on the planning board. Today, the Prospect Point Observation Tower is located in the park, and it, too, is about 300 feet tall. Across the river, though, the Skylon Tower rises 775 feet from the base of the falls.

Birdsill Holly, unlike many of his peers, had little to no interest in marketing, and because of this, he ended up being forgotten for most of the twentieth century. Although Holly's factory complex has been gone for more than a century (ironically, it burned down in a fire in 1909), fragments of it still remain and operate as the Lockport Cave, where the relatively unknown history of Holly and his innovations is retold to tourists from around the country. The cave is not a natural one, but it holds the remnants of the hydraulic raceway that Holly developed and designed to power his factory production off the excess water being diverted around the Erie Canal "Flight of Five" Locks located in the city. Luckily, Holly's inventions did stand the test of time, and the world is safer because of him.

3.

MARIA LOVE AND THE DAYCARE

C ities in the late 1800s, especially those in the North, were confronted with a number of growing social problems due to the country's industrialization, which included how to handle pollution and crime, as well as the rights of factory owners versus those of their laborers—a large portion of whom were women and children. This chapter describes the need for daycare for the children of working mothers and Maria Love's childcare solution, the Fitch Crèche, which was opened in 1881.

Prior to the Civil War, the country was growing by leaps and bounds. The population in 1820 was slightly less than 10 million. It had mushroomed to more than 50 million in 1880. Buffalo, too, was bursting due to its recognition as a successful international trading city. From 2,000 residents in 1820, to 18,000 by 1840, and 80,000 by 1860, Buffalo had quadrupled its population in just twenty years. By 1880, it had nearly doubled again to 155,000. Even as fast as the city's growth was, as the country teetered on the brink of war in 1860, there was a shortage of skilled labor to run its burgeoning factories and the other businesses rising to support this industry. One of the ways to counter this shortage was to use child labor. Although child labor was not uncommon in the trade, as apprentices, they were generally treated better than factory laborers. Long days in grueling conditions for low wages were only one of the problems the children faced before child labor laws were passed in 1938.

The factory labor shortage worsened when the Civil War started. Nearly three million soldiers served on both sides, and more than six hundred thousand of them lost their lives, not just in combat, but in the harsh conditions it caused. So, while the fighting continued, the northern factories required even more workers. Women picked up the slack. After the war, many women stayed in the work force. Part of this was due to necessity, but some of it, at least in New York State, was due to the Married Women's Property Act, which was passed by the state in 1848 and gave New York women the right to own property and keep their wages.

Although some women worked from their homes, providing sewing and washing services, many others worked outside the home, cleaning and cooking in the homes of the wealthy, as well as in mills and other factories. When women were away for work, their children—if they had children— were often left alone to fend for themselves. This meant that some of them got out of the house and wandered around, perhaps causing trouble in their neighborhoods. After one or two of these incidents, frustrated mothers sometimes took to locking their children in their homes. Such were the conditions confronting Maria Love as she grew into womanhood.

Maria (pronounced with a long "i" rather than the traditional "e") Maltby Love was born on January 26, 1840, on a farm in Clarence, New York to Thomas Cutter Love from Cambridge, Massachusetts, and Maria Maltby Love, from Hatfield, Connecticut. Her parents were married on November 17, 1824, and the family resided in Batavia, New York, for a number of years before moving west to Clarence. Her father was one of the first aldermen of the city of Buffalo and was a veteran who had fought and been wounded in the War of 1812. Prior to the Civil War, Maria's father was a staunch abolitionist, familiarizing her with the racial issues of the time. He later became a judge and a congressman, making her aware of the justice and legal systems as well. In addition to her father being a veteran, most of the men in Maria's life served in the military, including several uncles and both of her maternal and paternal grandfathers, who had fought in the Revolutionary and French and Indian wars.

Maria Love attended school in Buffalo, first at P.S. 10 and then at Central High, before going on to finish her studies out of state at the Farmington School for Girls in Connecticut. Because of her family background, Love grew up aware of social injustice, especially the negative effects of war, poor public education and racial issues. By the age of seventeen, she was already the secretary of the Ladies of the Industrial School, a group that raised funds and collected clothing for destitute children. In 1874, at the age of thirty-four, Maria was a chairman of a newly organized society that was chartered to raise funds for the construction of the *Soldiers and Sailors Monument*, which was unveiled in 1882. She was also known to run a small school out of her Delaware Avenue mansion.

Love was not alone in her drive for social justice. Many of Buffalo's citizens were early proponents of social activism. In 1853, New York City formed the Children's Aid Society to help poor and homeless children, and in 1873, Buffalo created its own Buffalo City Children's Aid Society. In 1877, the city leaders founded the Charity Organization Society, a coalition of all the city's charities, to help coordinate fundraising and equitably disperse aid. Based on a similar organization in London, this was the first such coalition in the United States and was later replicated around the country. Love was active in—or at least aware of—these charitable societies in Buffalo, and as part of her volunteering, she was often in single mother homes, where she would see evidence of malnutrition and other health issues in children. Although the city did have a "poor department" that provided some aid for those living in poverty, Love noticed that many people were afraid to apply for aid, and many were labeled as undeserving, so they were refused aid. She hoped to change the stigma attached to asking for help but was unsure of the best way to proceed.

On a trip to Paris, Love found her answer. She toured a French *crèche*, or "cradle school," that had been opened in 1844 by Firmin Marbeau. The crèche impressed Love and gave her a model of a way to both help working mothers and their families during working hours and also see to the children's medical and nutritional needs. She decided to open a crèche for the children of Buffalo. She started organizing it in 1877, gathering together a group of like-minded individuals who raised funds and looked for a suitable location for the crèche. In 1881, Maria Love opened the Fitch Crèche, which is generally acknowledged as the first daycare center in America, at 159 Swan Street in Buffalo, New York. Although there are claims that there were daycare centers in Boston as early as the 1840s and that there was a day "nursery" in New York City in 1854, Maria Love based her crèche on the one she had visited in Paris.

Love named her crèche after the owner of the building it occupied, Benjamin Fitch, a New York businessman who donated the building to Love. The building was three stories tall with a full basement. The first floor was for children ages four to seven and provided kindergarten education in a large classroom, as well as a playroom, dining room and bathrooms. The second floor was a nursery for infants, and on the third floor, there was an infirmary and sleeping quarters for the nurses. The basement held the matron's office, as well as the kitchen, dining room for employees, laundry room and storage rooms.

Left: Maria Love as a young woman. *Courtesy of the Maria M. Love Convalescent Fund Collection.*

Right: Sketch of Benjamin Fitch. *Courtesy of the* Buffalo Courier, *January 29, 1897.*

The average wage for factory workers at the time was $1.50 per day, and the Fitch Crèche allowed the children of disadvantaged working women to have professional childcare and education services while their mothers worked. The crèche also provided medical treatment for the children as needed. The modest fee for all of this was $0.05 per child per day, yet it was possible to waive the fee if needed. The justification for a fee—even one so low—was that the women recognized the crèche was not a charity, and they only brought children when they really had a job that day. In 1885, the crèche earned $296.60, and in 1896, it served an average of twenty-eight children per day, with a total of more than nine thousand for the year.

The 1885 *Harper's Monthly* article that was mentioned earlier in the Dart chapter included a glowing description of the crèche and some stunning illustrations. It also mistakenly noted that the crèche was based on one located in London, not Paris, and that it had opened in 1879, not 1881:

> *Think of having to take care of twenty thousand babies! This is what the Fitch Crèche has done since 1879. This great public cradle is the most interesting charity in Buffalo, because the most unique. Founded on the model of the London Day Nursery to care for little children whose mothers earn their support as char-women, it has so far outstripped its progenitor as to be called the model crèche of the world.*

A sketch of the Fitch Crèche. *Courtesy of* Leslie's Magazine, *1881.*

Love continued to receive good press about her crèche and was helping establish new ones as well. Some of this was aided by the 1893 Columbian Exposition in Chicago. An article about the construction of the fair in the January 7, 1893 issue of the *Illustrated American* discussed a highlight of the children's building:

> *An especially notable detail of the scheme will be the crèche, which will be under the direction of Miss Maria Love, who is at the head of the Fitch crèche at Buffalo, N.Y., generally regarded as the model nursery of the United States. She will take with her to Chicago a corps of trained nurses to assist her. Mothers with children in arms coming to the fair may leave them at the crèche while they go to visit the other buildings on the grounds. The idea is to take in each day possibly a hundred children, ranging from two months old to three years, and to illustrate by means of them the best methods of conducting a day nursery.*

When the Fitch Crèche was profiled in the January 29, 1897 issue of the *Buffalo Courier* as one of Buffalo's greatest charitable accomplishments, it had also implemented a training program for nursemaids. As the article stated:

Left: Dining in the Crèche. *Right*: Nursery in the Crèche. *Courtesy of* Harper's Magazine, *1885.*

The purpose and object of the crèche is many fold—the proper care of children and their primary instruction, the education of nursemaids, the finding of employment for mothers, and in general as wide as charity itself. In addition to their work in caring for the children left at the crèche, the nursemaids are instructed by means of a course of lectures on physiology, nursery science, physiology [sic] and disorders of digestion, the diet of children, the teeth, the skin and its influence on health, bathing, clothing and exercise, sleep and rest, common ailments, medication, emergencies and contagion. In addition to these lectures, the maids are instructed in cooking, laundry work and general housework, and in plain sewing, patching, and darning. When the nursemaid's work has been satisfactorily accomplished, she receives a diploma.

The article also mentions that the Charity Organization Society, which was the major funding source for the crèche, was planning on starting a second crèche, but it seems that never materialized. That same article included several illustrations of the crèche itself and one of its namesakes, Benjamin Fitch, which was shown earlier in this book.

Sketch of the Fitch Crèche. *Courtesy of the* Buffalo Courier, *January 29, 1897.*

In 1903, Love created a fund that is now known as the Maria Love Convalescent Fund to help women and children convalescing from health problems. It provided temporary funding to people who couldn't work and weren't eligible for other aid. This fund still exists today and has expanded from simple convalescent aid to include five types of individual assistance, such as medical-related transportation, medications, food for special diets

Opposite, top: Sketch of the kindergarten at the Fitch Crèche. *Courtesy of the* Buffalo Courier, *January 29, 1897.*

Opposite, bottom: Sketch of the nursery at the Fitch Crèche. *Courtesy of the* Buffalo Courier, *January 29, 1897.*

Right: A portrait of Maria Love in her later years. *Courtesy of the Maria M. Love Convalescent Fund Collection.*

and medical equipment. It also funds other charities, primarily those that support children. The money used by the fund is raised by a spring luncheon and a large annual ball, which was started the same year as the fund, more than one hundred years ago.

Maria Love died on July 20, 1931, at the age of ninety-one, and she was buried in Forest Lawn Cemetery. The crèche building outlasted her but was eventually demolished on June 28, 1998. Love never married or had children, but she operated the crèche for more than fifty years and inspired all those she worked with to continue her benevolence.

4.

ALFRED SOUTHWICK AND THE ELECTRIC CHAIR

T he social problems caused by the population growth and changing workforce of the late 1800s was conducive to an increase in major crime. This meant that society was also faced with the dilemma of what to do with the criminals. Although there were penitentiary systems, capital offenses were generally still punishable by death. In 1881, Alfred Southwick, a Buffalo dentist, invented the electric chair as a more humane alternative to hanging for those who were given a death sentence. This chapter describes the invention and explains the controversy it raised—and still raises—today.

Alfred Porter Southwick was born on May 18, 1826, in Saybrook, Ohio, in Ashtabula County. He was the oldest of the seven children of Abijah Southwick and Roxanna McDonald. He was educated in Ashtabula, and around 1852, Southwick went to work in Buffalo as an engineer at the Western Transit Company. Shortly thereafter, he was promoted to chief engineer.

Southwick's family records are confusing at best. Some state that he married Mary M. Flynn, who was born in Ireland, on May 26, 1853. However, other records indicate that a daughter, Mary R. Southwick, was born in Michigan six years earlier than that, around 1847, so it may have been that Mary Flynn was Southwick's second wife or that Southwick was Flynn's second husband. Whatever the actual sequence of family events, in 1855, Southwick began his studies in dentistry. He initially apprenticed with a local dentist but was still listed as an engineer residing at 13 North Connecticut Street in the 1861 and 1862 Buffalo city directories. He opened his dental practice at 280 Main Street in 1862. The Buffalo city directories started grouping professionals by

Alfred Southwick. *From the collection of Pamela Ferguson.*

occupation in 1864, and Southwick is one of the seventeen dentists listed.

Southwick's first invention was a medical device used to treat cleft palates, a disfiguring split in the roof of the mouth. In 1877, he was invited to speak at the annual meeting of the New York Dental Association to describe the device. After speaking with a variety of colleagues, Southwick realized that one of the drawbacks to dentistry was the pain it caused patients, so he started thinking about the possibility of using low-voltage electricity to minimize the pain.

Electricity came to his mind because it was starting to be harnessed to power machinery—much as steam had been a few decades earlier. With its proximity to Niagara Falls, Buffalo was one of the cities at the forefront of exploration with this new power source. It was leading the nation in other areas as well. By 1880, Frederick Olmsted and his partner Calvert Vaux had designed and implemented most of Buffalo's parks and parkways system, which was the largest they designed in the country. Bordering their park, now known as Delaware Park, the city also had a zoo, making it one of the oldest zoos in the United States.

During this time, there were at least nine major local newspapers: the *Buffalo Morning Express*, the *Buffalo Commercial*, the *Catholic Union*, the *Buffalo Courier*, the *Buffalo Times*, the *Buffalo Examiner*, the *Daily Christian Advocate*, the *Buffalo Evening News* and the *Buffalo Enquirer*, as well as some foreign-language newspapers. As was often the case in large cities, each of these newspapers gave slightly to wildly different versions of the current events of the day. It was the accounts of one specific event in these papers that helped Southwick create his next invention.

In August 1881, Southwick was intrigued by the death of a fellow Buffalo man named George Smith, who was electrocuted at the Brush Electric Light and Power Company, one of the first electric companies in the country. Brush Electric generated power for twelve streetlights on Buffalo's Ganson Street, and because of its novelty, the plant attracted a fair number of sightseers. Although the various newspaper reports differed greatly in their accounts, the gist of the incident was that the intoxicated thirty-year-old dock worker, George Smith, had reached over the fence around the plant and grabbed two copper generating brushes—one in each hand—thus completing an electric circuit, which then sent an electric current through his body. Some reports said Smith died instantly, while others said he lived briefly after the power was cut off. Regardless of the sequence, in the end, his hands needed to be pried from the brushes, yet his body showed no other signs of electrocution. As reported in the *New York Times*'s August 11, 1881 reprint from the August 8, 1881 *Buffalo Commercial Advertiser*:

> *He seized two strips, one in each hand. Instantly a circuit was formed, and he dropped on to the railing rigid. Only a gasp was heard as the man fell. His hands still grasped the strips, and Mr. Chaffee and the others rushed to his assistance found it impossible to loosen the clenched fists until the machine had been stopped and the current cut off. It was seen at once that Smith was dead....He was a healthy and strong man but succumbed to the powerful agency like an infant....All the organs were in normal condition, and it was found that the cause of the rashly curious man's sudden death was asphyxia, or paralysis of the nerves of respiration.*

In addition to appearing in the *New York Times*, Smith's death was so unusual that it was reported in more than fifty different newspapers, including those in Baltimore; Boston; Philadelphia; Washington, D.C.; Kansas City; Hartford; Harrisburg; and even Montgomery, Alabama. With his mind already considering electricity for reducing patients' pain during dentistry work, this event got Southwick thinking about electricity as a more humane form of capital punishment.

Shortly after Smith's death, Southwick learned that the State of New York was looking for alternatives to hanging, and Southwick, along with a colleague, Dr. George Fell, started to experiment on small animals to test his electrocution theories. Knowing that the local Society for the Prevention of Cruelty to Animals (SPCA) had many strays that were killed by drowning when not placed in new homes, the men convinced the SPCA to allow them to use electrocution on those animals instead.

One of the issues New York governor David Hill had used in his gubernatorial campaign was capital punishment, so shortly after his inauguration in 1886, he created a commission to study it. He appointed Southwick, Elbridge T. Gerry and Matthew Hall to that commission. Gerry was a lawyer, an active member of the New York Tammany Hall political regime, a founder of the Society for the Prevention of Cruelty to Children and the grandson of Elbridge Gerry, who served as the fifth vice-president of the United States. Not much is known about the commission's other member, Matthew Hall; he is usually simply listed as a resident of Albany, New York.

Sometimes referred to as the Gerry Commission, the panel of three did quite a bit of public outreach to poll opinions on capital punishment. At that time, "short drop" hanging was the method that was used, but very often, death took upward of twenty minutes. The commission approached people in the legal as well as medical fields and gathered more than two hundred responses to their inquiries as to the best method of execution; 40 percent of the respondents were in favor of keeping hanging as the state's method of execution while 44 percent thought that—as the panel had described electrocution—moving to electrocution would be the more humane approach. Other options that were considered but later discarded as inappropriate were the guillotine, the garrote and shooting via a firing squad. The commission's report was submitted in January 1888, and denigrators of the Gerry Commission's report started calling electrocution "Gerrycide."

As Southwick and the commission tried to decide on the appropriate level of voltage for electrocution, Southwick consulted Thomas Edison, who was well known in the Buffalo–Niagara Falls area. Edison, who it was later revealed was an opponent to capital punishment, told him to contact George Westinghouse instead. At that time, there was a bitter rivalry between Edison, a proponent of direct current (DC) and Westinghouse and Tesla, proponents of alternating current (AC). AC was winning at the time because it could be maintained over longer distances. Edison was intentionally trying to make AC look bad by having it associated with capital punishment. He, in fact, went so far as to demonstrate the dangers of AC by electrocuting helpless animals in public venues and calling the result being "Westinghoused." (The most spectacular was the murder of a circus elephant, which was filmed for posterity and can still be viewed. However, this happened in 1903, after Edison had already lost the current war, and it is unlikely that he was personally involved in either the electrocution itself or the filming of it.) Edison did, apparently, purchase used Westinghouse AC generators and gave them to prisons after Westinghouse refused to continue selling his generators to them. Still, the term electrocution won out, as did, ultimately, AC electric generation over DC generation.

New York's lawmakers agreed with the commission's recommendation and passed the state execution law later in 1888. The electricity was to be delivered using a specially designed wooden chair, which contained two electric lines. One line was in the base of the chair, which was to be attached

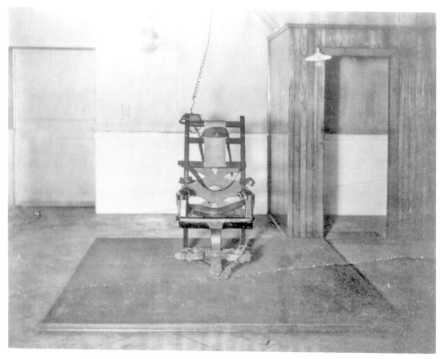

The electric chair at Auburn Prison. *Courtesy of the Library of Congress.*

to the prisoner's leg, and the second line went to the top of the chair, where it was attached to a metal bowl with a wet sponge that was placed on the prisoner's head. The process was designed to take place in two parts. The first shock of about one thousand volts was meant to kill the brain, and the longer but lower-voltage shock was meant to stop the heart.

The first execution under the new law was that of Buffalo resident William Kemmler, who had been convicted of murdering his lover, Tillie (Matilda) Ziegler, in their apartment at 526 South Division Street with thirty-one hatchet blows in March 1889. He was sentenced to death and was due to be executed in June 1889, but a series of unsuccessful appeals to the electrocution law delayed the execution. It finally took place on August 6, 1890, in Auburn State Prison. How well this first execution went is a matter of debate because it certainly did not proceed according to plan. Too low of a voltage was used on the first shock, so they gave him a higher-voltage shock that lasted, according to some witnesses, for more than four minutes. Of course, this was less than 20 percent of the time it often took someone to die by hanging, but the press didn't report it that way.

Illustration of Kemmler in the electric chair. *From* Kemmler; Or, The Fatal Chair. A Thrilling Detective Story, *1890.*

The Auburn Prison chair had been designed by Edwin Davis, who worked for the prison, and he later received a patent for the design. Some suggest that Thomas Edison should be credited with the invention, but in his slur campaign against AC, he did not use a chair. The *New York Tribune* ran nearly two full pages on the execution. The *Buffalo Courier* called it "Electricide" rather than electrocution, but that nomenclature did not last either. The media had a field day with the reports of the event—not all of which were accurate. The execution gained so much attention that the governor decided future executions would be held without media and that spectators would be under a gag order.

The succession of headlines from the August 6, 1890 issue of the *Buffalo Evening News* showed the amount of hype that was involved. The first headline simply read "Killed," and it was followed by "Kemmler Is Put to Death by the Electric Process," then "IT WAS AN AWFUL SIGHT." And as if those weren't enough, three more headlines followed, stating, "The Body Fumed as If Burning and Gave Off Sickening Odors," "THE PROCESS A FAILURE," and "Dr. Spitzka Says There Will Never Be Another Electrocution."

Despite these bad reviews, electrocution was ultimately seen as successful, and within a few years, most of the East Coast had adopted it as a form of capital punishment. But the controversy continued, and today, states that do carry out the death penalty use lethal injections rather than electrocution. Although Southwick helped found several local and state entities, including the School of Dentistry at the University at Buffalo, his dental business and his inventions did not give him the wealth that was enjoyed by many of his fellow innovators. He died on June 11, 1898, at his home at 456 Niagara Street. O.P. Gifford from the Delaware Avenue Baptist Church officiated his funeral, and his business partner, John Madden, inherited the business.

There is no local charity associated with Southwick's name, and most people who know who he was would like to forget what might be considered a stain on the city's reputation. But we need to remember the context of his invention, for he truly believed electrocution was a more humane punishment, and that sentiment fits in perfectly with the strong role Buffalo has played in promoting social reforms.

5.

LOUISE BETHUNE AND ARCHITECTURE

By 1880, Buffalo's population had mushroomed to more than 150,000. The influx of people and industry to the city required the construction of commercial buildings, homes and schools. This chapter discusses Louise Bethune, the first female Fellow of the American Institute of Architects (AIA), her architecture practice and how she paved the way for other female professionals.

Louise Bethune, whose given name was Jennie Lulu Blanchard, was born on July 21, 1856, in Waterloo, New York. Her parents were Emma Melona Williams and Dalson Wallace Blanchard; her father was a math teacher and the principal of the Waterloo Union School. Her family moved to Buffalo in 1866. Although she was homeschooled while in Waterloo, in Buffalo, some records indicate that Bethune attended Buffalo Female Academy and then Buffalo High School. When she graduated from Central High in 1874, her name was listed as J. Lulu Blanchard, and she continued to use Jennie as her legal name. But sometime after graduation, she started appearing in the press under the first name of Louise.

As it has been noted in previous chapters, during this time, Buffalo was experiencing phenomenal growth as a transportation hub. The Erie Canal was still very active, and the railroads were developing as well. The improved transportation systems brought even more residents who needed homes, schools and business buildings. The Blanchard family had moved to Buffalo because of the city's need for teachers in those schools, and Louise Bethune was eager to accommodate the needs for the buildings.

Louise Bethune. *From Chuck LaChiusa's collection.*

Bethune embarked on her architectural career in 1876, when she started as a draftsman for Buffalo architect Richard A. Waite. Architecture, as a stand-alone profession, was relatively new, so there were not as many barriers to women who were entering the field as there were to the older professions of doctors and lawyers, and although the first U.S. architectural schools opened in the late nineteenth century (MIT in 1868, Cornell in 1871 and Columbia in 1881) the Ecole des Beaux-Arts in Paris was still considered the premier architectural school in Bethune's era. Most American architects were not able to afford the sojourn abroad, so they worked as draftsmen for other architects, as Bethune did.

Her mentor, Richard Waite, was born in England on May 14, 1848, and his family moved to the United States in 1856. They lived in New York City for a while before moving to Buffalo. When Bethune worked for Waite, the firm designed Dr. Pierce's Palace Hotel, a massive 250-room sanitarium overlooking Lake Erie that was completed in 1878. It was purportedly the first building in Buffalo with telephones and an elevator, but it burned down three short years later in 1881. Waite went on to be credited as the first American architect to design government buildings in Canada, including the Ontario Legislative Building in Toronto.

Bethune worked in Waite's office for five years and became his assistant in the later years of their work together. In October 1881, while attending the ninth congress of the Association for the Advancement of Women, which was held in Buffalo, Bethune announced that she was starting her own business. The next month, she purchased a property on Porter from her mother (using her legal name of Jennie Blanchard), and on December 10 of that same year, she married Robert A. Bethune, a colleague in Waite's office, and together, they launched their new architecture firm, R.A. & L. Bethune.

Robert Bethune was born on June 7, 1855, in Bowmansville, Ontario, Canada, and immigrated to the United States with his family in 1861. After studying architecture in Detroit, he moved to Buffalo and met his soon-to-be wife at the Waite offices, where they were both employed. The Bethunes had one child, a son named Charles W. Bethune, who was born in 1883.

It is important to remember that, in this era, it was uncommon for women to work. When the Bethunes started their firm in 1881, only about 14 percent of American women worked outside the home, whereas 90 percent of men did. And the majority of these men, approximately 60 percent, still worked in agricultural jobs, not urban ones. So, the Bethunes were unique on both fronts.

One of the Bethunes' larger jobs early in their careers was the Seventy-Four Regiment Armory, which was built for the regiment's drilling practices and arms storage. The large Romanesque-style building was finished in 1886, but it was replaced within three years by the larger Connecticut Street Armory. The Bethune building became the Elmwood Music Hall on the corner of Elmwood and Virginia Streets, and it functioned as Buffalo's main music venue until 1940.

Louise Bethune was not only a pioneer in her profession, but in her hobbies as well. She was a member in the local genealogical society. Several of the club meetings were held at her home at 215 Franklin Street. She was also an active bicycler, and in 1888, she was one of the founders of the Buffalo Women's Wheel Club. The club changed its name to the Women's Wheel and Athletic Club in 1889, but in December 1896, the club voted to dissolve. As the last president noted in a *Buffalo Commercial* article, "When it was organized several years ago…it was the first women's wheeling club in the world, but now, all women are awheel, and the objects of the club were at an end." There were about forty members at that time, and Bethune was still a director of the group when it folded. It held its last official meeting in January 1897.

Armory/Elmwood Music Hall. *From the author's collection.*

As the architecture field continued to grow in the late 1800s, two large architect associations were created in the United States. The first was the American Institute of Architects (AIA), which was founded in 1857 and headquartered in Washington, D.C. The second was the Western Association of Architects (WAA), which was founded in 1884 and headquartered in Chicago. The WAA was founded because there was a perceived East Coast and Midwest divide among the architects who were practicing at that time, but as Buffalo architects were located between the two, they were active in both associations. In 1885, Bethune applied to join the WAA. Prominent Midwest architects Daniel Burnham and Louis Sullivan, both of whom later designed outstanding Buffalo buildings, recommended her to the rest of the board, and she was admitted to the association.

The following year, Louise Bethune helped create a local architecture group that was known at that time as the Buffalo Society of Architects. In 1887, she was elected as the first vice-president of that local group. By 1889, the WAA and the AIA had resolved their differences and found it prudent to merge. Although all the male architects in the WAA received their Fellow designations in the AIA when the two organizations merged, sources are mixed on whether or not the Fellow designation was also awarded to Bethune at that time. Not well known today—but influential both locally and nationally during the merger—was Buffalo architect

POLICE STATION NO. 8 AT EAST BUFFALO.

Architect's sketch of Buffalo Police Station Number 8. *Courtesy of the* Buffalo Morning Express, *April 23, 1887.*

William Worth Carlin. Carlin was very active in both the WAA and the AIA and played a pivotal role in the merger of the two groups. He defeated Daniel Burnham for the WAA presidency in 1888, and Bethune served as Carlin's second vice-president. Carlin was also the president of the New York architect's association and the vice-president of the merged AIA and WAA under Richard Morris Hunt. He helped standardize contracts and fee rates that were used nationally, so it is unlikely that he would have allowed Bethune to not receive her FAIA with the rest of the group.

Apparently, sometime in late 1890 or early 1891, the Bethunes made their longtime draftsman, William R. Fuchs, a partner in the company, and the firm became known as Bethune, Bethune & Fuchs. There is some confusion as to the date on which this happened, as Fuchs submitted his own drawings to the Erie County Bank competition in 1890, and the Bethunes did not, but by October 1890, Bethune and Fuchs were reported to be designing a $10,000 home for W.J. Conners on the corner of Tifft Street and White's Corners Road. By May 1891, the name had formally changed. Later in 1891, the Bethunes purchased a block of five buildings between Franklin and Pearl Streets to "be modernized," and they turned the house on the corner of Huron and Franklin Streets into their office.

The firm continued to land large, important jobs, but still, women in the field were rare. As Bethune herself put it in an 1891 address titled "Women and Architecture":

The professions of medicine and law were far advanced before the much-needed and highly appreciated woman physician and lawyer appeared. Women have entered the architectural profession at a much earlier stage of its existence, even before it has received legislative recognition. They meet no serious opposition from the profession nor the public. Neither are they warmly welcomed. They minister to no special needs of women and receive no special favors from them.

In that 1890 to 1892 time frame, the firm was commissioned to design the new Livestock Exchange Building, which was constructed on William Street; the Lockport High School; an extension to the Erie County Prison; and seven homes and stables, including a mansion near Lockport, New York, for the renowned "Seven Sutherland Sisters." The Livestock Exchange was located near the preexisting meatpacking plants and slaughterhouses. The resulting stockyard area covered nearly one hundred acres of the city and was purported to be the largest in the United States east of Chicago and the fifth largest in the world. The building was a three-story brick, Romanesque-style structure with a five-story tower, and it is no longer extant. The Sutherland Mansion, which was left abandoned for decades, burned down in 1938. The Bethunes discussed the construction of a fourteen-story building in local publications as well, but that didn't seem to materialize.

In the February 9, 1892 issue of the *Buffalo Enquirer*, an article titled "A Clever Woman's Work" talks about Bethune's designs and her bicycling:

Mrs. Louise Bethune of this city is a very successful architect. And that does not mean that she is simply able to design and do office work, although she is proficient in this difficult line. But Mrs. Bethune does all that a capable, practical architect is expected to do. She handles all the dwelling houses that come to the office of the firm of which she is a member. Designs, makes estimates and directs the work. More than half of her time is spent in personally superintending the building.

She goes from place to place on her bicycle, which she finds to be a great convenience. Mrs. Bethune is full of ideas, clever and well-read. She devotes herself almost entirely to her work, rarely going out "on pleasure bent" and finds her lot a very happy and satisfactory one.

In addition to being an outspoken proponent of cycling, Bethune was also outspoken about payment for architects. The professional groups she was active in made great strides in the late nineteenth and early twentieth centuries for equitable pay, and one of the ways in which this was accomplished was the minimization of participation in design competitions that did not pay. Not surprisingly, she was especially vocal about not participating in the design competition for the buildings for the Chicago World's Columbian Exposition, which was held in 1893. Her male counterparts received $10,000 for their designs, yet the women were only allowed to design the Woman's Building, and that was a competition with a mere $1,000 prize. So, Bethune did not participate, and she urged her female colleagues to do the same.

Locally, the 1890s were full of building projects in the city, despite the Panic of 1893, and these were attracting many noted Chicago-based architects. Burnham and Sullivan, who had promoted Bethune's membership in the WAA more than a decade earlier, both designed landmark buildings in Buffalo in 1896. The Burnham-designed building is the Ellicott Square Building, a ten-story-tall nearly 450,000-square-foot full-block structure that was the world's largest office building when it opened. The Sullivan-designed building is the Guaranty Building, and it was also known as the Prudential Building. Similar to, but much more ornate than, Sullivan's 1891 Wainwright Building in St. Louis, the terra-cotta Guaranty Building is thirteen stories tall and is often noted as a pioneer in skyscrapers.

Bethune was vocal about not bringing in these outside architects to work in the city, and despite her disdain for competitions, the firm did enter them,

Buffalo Livestock Exchange. *From the author's collection.*

especially in the late 1890s. They submitted a design for the Maston Park High School in 1895, as well as for the Buffalo Savings Bank in 1897, but did not win either competition. During this time, they also designed two factories, the grandstands for the Buffalo Baseball Association, a grocery store, three houses and a power transformer building—purportedly for Nikola Tesla—to supply electricity for the trolleys. They apparently completed the remodeling of the block of buildings they'd purchased in 1891 as well, which, except for the one they'd retained for their office, were sold in 1898 for $30,000.

In 1897, Buffalo won the bid to host the next World's Fair, but it was postponed due to the Spanish-American War. Planning for the 1901 Pan-American Exposition began in earnest in 1899. Heralded as the largest national event since the war had ended, the festivities attracted permanent residents and millions of visitors. At this time, the city was the eighth largest in the country, with more than 350,000 residents. It had electric lights, about three hundred miles of paved macadam roads, an extensive Olmsted-designed park system and twenty-eight railroad lines. Buffalo was the world's largest grain port, largest lumber port, second-largest cattle market and sixth-largest overall port. Its cultural amenities included two libraries and nine theaters.

Bethune, Bethune & Fuchs designed a meat plant building for Jacob Dold at 145 Swan Street in 1901. It was a four-story brick-and-frame building, approximately thirty thousand square feet in size, just down the block from the Fitch Crèche. Dold never occupied the building, however, and from 1906 to 1933, it was the corporate headquarters for the Witkop & Holmes chain of grocery stores. This building is still extant and is listed in the National Register of Historic Places.

The firm's magnum opus, the Lafayette Square Hotel, was also designed in this time frame. A seven-story white terra cotta and red brick building on the corner of Clinton and Washington Streets, the hotel was opened in 1904. Originally planned to have 225 rooms to help hold the millions of visitors for the 1901 Pan-American Exhibition, financing and other delays postponed its completion. The style is considered to be French Renaissance, and it was purported to be one of the best hotels in the United States when it opened because each room boasted not only hot and cold running water in private bathrooms but a telephone as well.

The interior of the hotel was spectacular. The main ballroom had crystal chandeliers, leaded-glass skylights, marble columns and paneling of mahogany and oak abounded. The Lafayette Hotel was a premier hotel for more than fifty years, but as that section of the city declined, so did the hotel,

Lafayette Hotel. *From the author's collection.*

and it eventually became a dismal boardinghouse. It was rescued in 2012 and is now an apartment building, boutique hotel and banquet venue. It is also listed in the National Register of Historic Places.

Although the opening of the Lafayette Hotel was significant for the city and the firm, after its completion, there was a building slump in Buffalo. Robert Bethune was asked about the dearth of building projects in a 1905 interview in the *Buffalo Sunday Morning News*; the following are his comments:

> *I cannot recall a time in Buffalo when there was as little building in the downtown section of the city as there is at the present time. Up to a short time ago, there was none at all, but now, the work of running the White building up to 10 stories, together with the extension of the Manufacturers and Traders Bank, has broken upon the building calm. Further up Main Street, the Wilson business block is going up at Main and Tupper Streets, and now, it is announced that Aug. 1 [sic] will see the start of the new chamber of commerce building, so it will not be so poor a building year in the business district as it promised to be, but it is not what it has been in late years.*
>
> *There is no particular reason for this. Every city experiences a period of building depression every now and then and then along comes another boom. Out in the residential sections, there is plenty of building of all*

kinds, and some handsome residences are going up, along with many of the more ordinary kind. Several industries are erecting plants, too, notably the Bisulfate of Lime Company and the Metropolitan Silk Company, and these are what Buffalo wants.

Compared with Cleveland, Pittsburg, Toledo and other cities of the Middle West, building in Buffalo is quiet just now. But nobody need to worry over that. Buffalo has a great future before her. It's bound to come, and it's coming right along.

It is interesting that 1905 yielded only one known project for the firm: the Wilson Building. The building was a collection of stores that occupied 695–705 Main Street. Just three years later, some say Louise Bethune retired from active practice, but she still paid attention to the architecture field. In a 1909 interview, she reiterated her concern about bringing outside architects to Buffalo. "I do not believe in competitions among architects any more than I would favor competitions among physicians for the care of a patient. I believe in confining all business possible to Buffalo, as the best means of promoting the interest of the city. Some people believe that anything which comes from another city must necessarily be better than anything we have here. That is one of the things that is the 'matter with Buffalo.'"

Jennie Lulu (Louise) Blanchard Bethune died from kidney failure on December 18, 1913, at only fifty-seven years of age. Her funeral was held at the Bethunes' home at 904 Tonawanda Street. Her obituary noted that she'd retired around 1911, but her will confirms the 1908 date. Robert died not quite two years later, on July 17, 1915. His funeral was also held at their home, and they were both buried in a single plot in Forest Lawn Cemetery. In an odd twist, however, the joint grave they shared carried only Robert's name and dates of birth and death. Whether it was a cost-saving measure is not known, but in 2013, on the centennial anniversary of her death, the local, State of New York and National AIA leadership decided that they needed to rectify the matter. They purchased, engraved and installed a new headstone containing her name and dates of birth and death.

Louise Bethune was both conventional and unconventional. Her frequent listings in the social pages referred to her as Mrs. Robert A. Bethune, not by her first name—as was the custom. Yet she managed to create nearly 150 known building designs. However, as was often the case, not all of the buildings were constructed. As a daughter of teachers, she helped improve

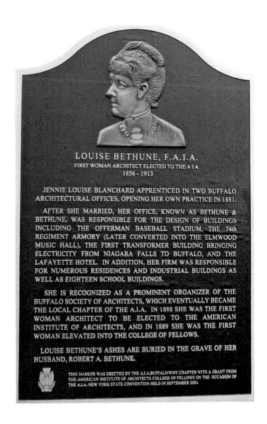

Bethune plaque in Forest Lawn Cemetery. *From the author's collection.*

education by designing eighteen schools. Perhaps due to her belief that local work should be performed by local business professionals, Bethune apparently did not design any buildings outside the western New York area. She was an outspoken supporter for women's rights but was also concerned about charity, education, health and safety. She designed sturdy, functional buildings that stood the test of time, while she also built the foundation for women in all professions.

6.

WILLIS CARRIER AND AIR CONDITIONING

Buffalo Forge, a large manufacturing company headquartered in Buffalo, was asked, in 1902, to help a company in Brooklyn solve an alignment problem with their printing presses. Willis Carrier created a device that removed the humidity in the air around the press, and later, he recognized the potential of this air-cooling apparatus. This chapter describes Carrier's invention, his founding of Carrier Engineering Company and the effect air conditioning has had on the world.

Willis Haviland Carrier was born in Angola, New York, just south of Buffalo, on November 26, 1876. His parents were Duane Williams Carrier and Elizabeth Haviland, a Quaker who married Carrier outside of her faith. After a stint as postmaster in Angola, Carrier's father decided to become a farmer. Carrier was their only child, but his grandparents and great-aunt also lived with the family, so he was surrounded by adults who were ready to teach him whatever he was interested in. He tended to make up his own games, which leaned toward machines and equipment. His mother died when he was only eleven, but she had taught him a problem-solving method to work with fractions, which he used throughout his life. After she passed away, he helped his father by milking the cows, delivering the milk and then walking to school. His father was remarried, in 1893, to Eugenia Adelaide Tifft.

Carrier attended Angola Academy in his hometown and graduated in 1894, in the middle of the 1893 Panic. (It is important to note that several sources say he graduated 1893, but the announcement of his graduation is in the June 21, 1894 *Buffalo Weekly Express*.) Although the panic did not affect Buffalo as much as other cities—especially those in the West and Midwest—the economic downturn did keep Carrier from furthering his education right away. Instead, he started teaching at a local school. The family home in Angola went into foreclosure in 1896, and Carrier moved in with his stepbrother in Buffalo. Then, he attended Buffalo's Central High, where he received an oration award for his talk on the "Sun-God" and graduated in June 1897.

Later in 1897, Carrier came in second in a scholarship "exam" for a free course at Cornell University, New York's land grant college. He registered as a freshman that fall and then won a two-year scholarship of $200 per year. Tuition at that time was $100 to $150 per year, but living expenses were estimated to cost another $300 to $500 per year. In the spring of 1898, he was on the short list for new freshmen who were likely to earn a spot on Cornell's rowing crew, which he did. He was six feet six inches tall and was active in other sports at Cornell as well, including basketball. He continued to teach and coach and do other odd jobs to supplement the stipend he received as part of his scholarship, and, as the story goes, in his senior year, he started a co-op laundry service with a classmate.

Carrier graduated from Cornell in 1901 with a degree in electrical engineering. As legend has it, he had hoped to land a job at General Electric, but no offer came, so he took an interview at Buffalo Forge. On the streetcar ride to that interview, he asked a fellow commuter for directions to the plant, and it turned out that the man he asked was an engineer there, J. Irvine Lyle, who later had a significant impact on Carrier and his career. Carrier was offered the job and started on July 1, 1901, with a wage of ten dollars a week.

Buffalo, in 1901, was the second-largest city in New York and the eighth largest in the country, with a population of more than 350,000 people. When Carrier started his job, the city was also in the midst of hosting the 1901 Pan-American Exposition, a seven-month-long World's Fair that had started on May 1 and continued until November 2. During that time, approximately 8 million people descended on the city to view a history of the world to date and the technology of the future. Some of this future-oriented technology included the extensive use of electric lights to decorate the exteriors of many of the buildings and the newly invented X-ray machine.

As its name implies, Buffalo Forge manufactured forges, but it also made industrial fans, drill machines, steam engines and heating equipment. Carrier was put to work on some of the heating-related commissions but

Willis H. Carrier. *Courtesy of Carrier Engineering, 1919.*

shortly discovered that the data he was relying on was flawed. After work hours, he gathered his own data and designed a more effective fan, which he presented to management late in 1901. The prevailing story is that management was so impressed that, in January 1902, he was given his own research department at double his original salary. Some of his earliest improvements were to dryers for lumber and coffee beans.

In the spring of that same year, his colleague J. Irvine Lyle, whom he'd met on the way to his interview the previous year and who was then working out of Buffalo Forge's Manhattan sales office, heard about a four-color printing problem at the Sackett & Wilhelms Lithography and Printing Company in Brooklyn, New York. Four-color printing was achieved by passing the paper through the machinery four separate times, and using the different color inks in the high humidity of New York City's summers was causing the passes to misalign. It was ruining the product and slowing down production. Lyle referred the problem to his friend Carrier, who postulated that he could mechanically manipulate the dew point of water to keep humidity in the press at a steady 55 percent, regardless of the season. By the end of the summer, the equipment was installed and working. Later that same summer, on August 29, 1902, Carrier married Edith Claire Seymour, a teacher and fellow 1901 Cornell graduate, and in October, they moved into their home at 120 Vermont Street.

There had been quite a bit of work done on refrigeration and humidity control before Carrier's time. It is said that in the 1500s, Leonardo Da Vinci created a water-based fan to cool down the bedroom of one of his patrons. Closer to modern times, in 1840, Dr. John Gorrie, who treated yellow fever patients, had developed a type of refrigeration to cool them down. Nearly thirty-five years later, Carl von Linde, in Munich, Germany, also built a refrigeration unit. The following year, Stuart Cramer created a system to help humidity levels in the cotton mills of the South, increasing their production by about one-third. It was Cramer who coined the term "air conditioning," but it was Carrier who earned the title of the "Father of Air Conditioning."

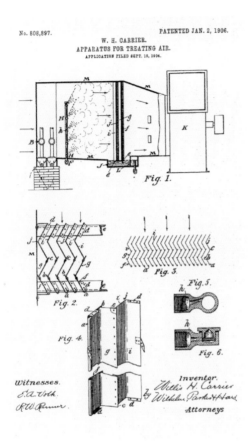

Carrier patent. *Courtesy of the United States Patent and Trademark Office.*

Why did he earn this title? He earned it because his patent for an "Apparatus for Treating Air" granted in 1906 (#808897) could both humidify and dehumidify air, and that differentiation is considered to be the start of the modern air conditioning era. Using a spray of water, his invention heated the water to humidify and cooled the water to dehumidify. As Dart was before him, Carrier was ridiculed by many in his field, but his technology proved reliable and ultimately revolutionized the world.

The first local office building purportedly designed specifically for air conditioning was the Larkin Administration Building, which was designed by Frank Lloyd Wright in 1902 and opened in 1904. The Larkin Company was an innovator in its own right, pioneering the notion of frequent purchaser premiums, especially in the form of high-end furniture. The company turned to Wright to create an iconic, future-oriented corporate headquarters that was the first to use many things common in today's office buildings, but Wright himself was very proud of the introduction of air conditioning in the building. As he noted in his 1955 book, *An American Architecture*, "It is interesting that I, an architect supposed to be concerned with the aesthetic sense of the building, should have…adopted many other innovations like the glass door, steel furniture, air-conditioning and radiant or 'gravity heat.' Nearly every technological innovation used today was suggested in the Larkin Building in 1904." Although several historians state that the air conditioning in the Larkin Building was ineffective—and that Wright was not the first to use it—Wright continued to claim it as one of his firsts. And many new buildings followed suit.

In 1905, Carrier became the manager of Buffalo Forge's engineering department, and he continued to refine his air inventions. After an installation at Chronicle Cotton Mills in Belmont, North Carolina, Carrier realized that machines and people could also affect the air, which meant he needed to adjust the system to introduce more water than he had originally calculated. Other installations included those at the pharmaceutical giant Parke Davis's building, as well as the Huguet Silk Mill and the Fuji Silk Spinning Company in Yokohama, Japan.

William W. Wendt was the owner of Buffalo Forge and the father of Margaret Wendt, whose foundation is another large philanthropic benefactor in Buffalo today. By 1907, Buffalo Forge was doing quite a bit of air conditioning–related business, and Lyle and Carrier suggested to Wendt that Buffalo Forge should create a subsidiary company just for the air conditioning applications. In early 1908, the Carrier Air Conditioning Company of America (CACCA) began operations, with Wendt listed as treasure and Carrier as vice-president. Requests for air conditioning were still coming in from textile and flour mills and heritage companies like American Tobacco Company, but they were also coming in for newer businesses, such as the Gillette Safety Razor Company and the Celluloid Company, which produced motion-picture film. Gillette was especially concerned with lowering humidity to keep its razor blades from rusting.

CACCA logo. *Courtesy of the Montgomery Advertiser, September 3, 1916.*

As noted previously, although there were refrigeration units long before Carrier—and even though the term "air conditioning" was coined before him—it is this notion of humidity control that differentiated Carrier's innovations. Experts in the field claim that there are four components to fully qualify as air conditioning; temperature control, humidity control, air circulation and ventilation control and air cleaning. Carrier conquered the humidity control aspect by controlling the dew point. He applied for a patent of this technology in 1907, and it was granted on February 3, 1914 (#1085971).

Today, the general population thanks Carrier for the cooling effects of air conditioning, but to his peers, his greatest achievement was his "epic" document "Rational Psychrometric Formulae," which he read to the 1911 convention of the American Society of Mechanical Engineers (ASME). Prior to this, much of the data and formulae associated with air conditioning calculations were gathered and deduced from special air conditions known as dry-bulb, wet-bulb and dew-point temperatures. Based on his own data, Carrier postulated four "rules" for air conditioning that are still true today. His formulae and data were therefore referred to as the "Magna Carta of air conditioning."

In the midst of these stellar professional accomplishments, Carrier was having personal issues. His father was killed by a Pierce-Arrow test vehicle in 1908 while crossing a Buffalo street. He lost his first wife on January 12, 1912, and then on April 16, 1913, he remarried. His new wife was Jennie Tifft Martin; she was also a schoolteacher and his stepsister. They resided at 1350 Amherst. The following year, he was elected to Cornell's honorary science club.

For the next few years, CACCA continued to be successful, but the tide was about to turn. When Buffalo Forge closed CACCA is in question, but the most common story is that, in 1914, with World War I looming, management decided to close the air conditioning subsidiary, so Lyle and Carrier decided to start their own firm. However, newspaper articles and advertisements showed that the CACCA logo continued to be used in late 1916 and well into the late 1920s. Buffalo Forge's annual meetings were advertised as including Carrier Air Conditioning people.

Regardless of how the parting actually occurred, in late 1914, Carrier traveled to New York City to meet with Lyle and Edward Murphy from the Philadelphia office. On June 26, 1915, Carrier, Lyle, Murphy and four other Buffalo Forge engineers, Edmond Heckel, L. Logan Lewis, Ernest T. Lyle and Alfred E. Stacy Jr., incorporated as the Carrier Engineering Corporation. The new company was often referred to as the Carrier Engineering Company (instead of Corporation), and it was headquartered at 39 Cortland Street in New York City. A profile of the new company and a detailed description of the roles of each of the principals appeared in the 1915 edition of *Textile World*. The publication also mentioned how the air conditioning jobs were to be divided between the new company and Buffalo Forge:

> *This new company will take over all of the special air conditioning work of the Carrier Air Conditioning Co., including all applications of the latter company's machines to the various industries requiring humidifying, dehumidifying or humidity regulation.*
>
> *The sale of Carrier air washers has been given to the sales organization of the Buffalo Forge Co. to be handled in the future with their fan and heating apparatus.*

So, standard applications that simply required the installation of existing equipment stayed with Buffalo Forge, while anything that required customized engineering went with the Carrier Engineering Company. In 1919, the company released an extensive book (over sixty pages) titled *Weather*; it was a compendium of photographs and stories of the company's numerous client applications to date. The book also introduced a mascot called the Mechanical Weatherman, who was noted on the title page as the author of the book. He noted that he could make weather to order and described his creation as follows: "An artist made me by endowing a control valve, or some such thing, with a pair of legs, a pair of arms, and a smile." He also explained that his job—and the company's—was to make "every day a good day" by creating whatever weather conditions a client needed. The book also showed schematic-like diagrams of how some of the more common units worked.

Advertisements for the company and its air conditioning installations in the *Refrigerating Engineering and Chemical Engineering Catalogue* continued to list its Cortland Street address until 1921, when the new corporate headquarters was listed as being in Newark, New Jersey. It was at this plant that, in May 1922, Carrier introduced what was known as the centrifugal refrigeration machine, also called a chiller. The first sales and installations of the new chiller were to two candy companies: W.F. Schrafft and Sons Candy near Boston and Stephen F. Whitman & Son in Philadelphia. The Schrafft company had been working with Carrier since 1917, when it had moved into a much larger facility and was having trouble with both heat and humidity. Too much heat was making chocolate "bloom," and too much humidity was melting the hard candies. They continued to upgrade their equipment as Carrier updated his products.

Left: The Mechanical Weatherman character. *Courtesy of* Carrier Engineering, *1919.*

Below: Carrier schematic. *Courtesy of* Carrier Engineering, *1919.*

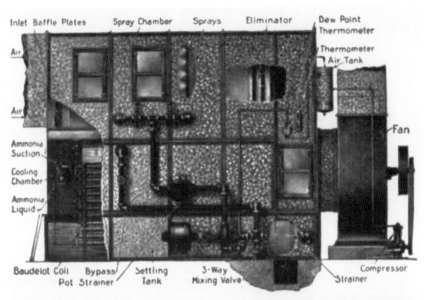

ILLUSTRATING A TYPICAL CARRIER INSTALLATION

Throughout the 1920s, Carrier installed additional chillers in large retail stores, such as Hudson's in Detroit and others in New York City, Boston and Dallas. The company also installed air conditioning in theaters, which used a different technology. Rather than cool from the floor, theater units cooled from the ceiling—much like modern air conditioning. These units were installed in Rivoli's Theatre in Manhattan, Grauman's Chinese Theatre in Los Angeles and the Palace Theatre in Dallas. Creameries, bakeries, breweries, meat plants and hospitals all requested and received air conditioning units, as did Madison Square Garden in 1925, which purchased air conditioning for the building and other units for the ice for the hockey rink.

Skyscrapers were also being designed to use air conditioning. The first was the T.W. Patterson Building in Fresno in 1926, followed by the Milam Building in San Antonio in 1928. Mines, ships and railroad cars were all being outfitted, both nationally and internationally. By 1929, the company had offices in Paris, London, Calcutta and Tokyo, and it continued to expand globally for the next two decades. In the 1930s, the seventy-story RCA Building at Rockefeller Center in New York City was constructed with dehumidifiers and centrifugal refrigerating units. It is said that the Rockefeller Center dehumidifiers removed water from the air at a rate of seven hundred gallons per hour and that the contract was for $1 million dollars. In the 1940s, four of New York City's tallest buildings were all cooled with Carrier equipment.

With the great strides being taken at the commercial level, Carrier was also introducing residential units. Carrier's first home installation took place in 1914 at the Charles Gates Mansion in Minneapolis, Minnesota, but by 1926, the company had created a more compact unit for "normal" homes. The ubiquitous window air conditioners of today, however, were not designed by Carrier; they were designed by H.H. Schultz and J.Q. Sherman in 1931. However, their units were too expensive for wide use at the time, and other inventors continued to make them smaller and cheaper.

In 1930, Carrier Engineering Company merged with two other companies, York Heating & Ventilating and Brunswick-Kroeschell, to become Carrier Corporation. By 1937, Carrier had five different plants operating around the country, and it decided to consolidate operations to a large common campus in Syracuse.

On the personal side, on June 3, 1939, Jennie Tifft Martin Carrier passed away at the age of seventy-two. Carrier remarried on February 7, 1941, this time to Elizabeth March Wise. Willis Carrier himself died on October 7, 1950. He and his three wives are buried in Buffalo's Forest Lawn Cemetery.

The company he founded continued to prosper after his death. It installed the air conditioning for both World Trade Center towers, as well as the Sears Tower. It was purchased by United Technologies in July 1979, and Carrier's legacy lives on and is reflected in modern society. People could not live and work in hot climates prior to air conditioning, and indoor hockey and figure skating did not exist. The distribution of the

1936 Carrier advertisement. *From the author's collection.*

U.S. population shifted south and west. The percentage of the country living in the "Sunbelt" increased from approximately 10 percent in 1900 to 28 percent by 1950 to 40 percent by 2000. Ironically, this migration was partially responsible for the disintegration of industry in the northern "Rustbelt" cities, including Buffalo.

7.

GLENN CURTISS AND AIRPLANES

Glenn Curtiss, an airplane inventor, opened a large plant in Buffalo in 1915. By 1918, Curtiss had expanded to more than 120,000 square feet worth of plants in the area and employed eighteen thousand workers. These plants continued to expand into the 1940s and were major contributors to America's World War II efforts. This chapter outlines Curtiss's rarely acknowledged role in aviation history, as well as his other inventions: air boats and travel trailers.

Glenn Curtiss's great-grandfather Gideon moved to Niagara County in Western New York from Litchfield, Connecticut, in 1817. Some sources state that Gideon was the first European settler in the small town of Ransomville, New York. Gideon's son, Glenn Curtiss's grandfather, was Claudius G. Curtiss, a Methodist minister who moved around western New York to a number of small churches. Gideon's grandson Frank Richmond Curtiss was born in 1854 and married Lua Andrews, his father's organist, in 1876. When Claudius was moved again from Jasper, NY to Hammondsport, NY, Frank and Lua moved there with them, and were married.

Their son, Glenn Hammond Curtiss, was born on May 21, 1878. He was so named because of his mother's love for the glen near their home and the founder of their village, Lazarus Hammond. In 1879, Reverend Curtiss was transferred back to Niagara County—this time, to Cambria, New York—but Frank and Lea remained in their beloved Hammondsport. In 1881, Reverend Curtiss retired and moved back to Hammondsport but died the next year. Unfortunately, in 1883, Frank also died, purportedly of "inflammation of the stomach," leaving the fledgling Glenn Curtiss's nurturing to his mother and grandmother.

One of Curtiss's favorite pastimes as a child was to listen to his grandmother Ruth read him "Darius Green and His Flying Machine," an epic poem about the misadventures of a young boy trying to fly. It was written by John T. Trowbridge, who Ruth had met in her youth, and it was republished in the *School, College and Public Reader* in 1876. It was also published in a lavishly illustrated booklet. The poem ends as follows:

> *And this is the moral,—Stick to your sphere.*
> *Or if you insist, as you have the right,*
> *On spreading your wings for a loftier flight,*
> *The moral is,—Take care how you light.*

As Curtiss and his grandmother laughed at the possibility of flight, little did either know how prophetic that poem would turn out to be.

Much of what is known about Curtiss's early years comes from a full-page profile of him that was published in the September 19, 1909 issue of the *New York Times*. According to that article, Curtiss's first "invention" was a modified hand-sled he created when he was ten or eleven to win a downhill race against another youth. When he was a year or two older, he was a newspaper carrier and wanted a "velocipede," as bicycles were originally called, but he could not afford one, so he built his own out of old buggy wheels. As the article stated:

> *The result was the production of a very unusual and most ungainly vehicle made of an old buggy wheel and some pieces of gas pipe. To the astonishment of everybody save the boy himself, who had confidence in the idea, this crudely constructed thing went....In a short time, he was giving trick exhibitions in the streets of the village for the amusement of the natives.*

In 1889, Curtiss's mother and younger sister, Rutha, moved to Rochester so that Rutha could attend the new school for the deaf that had been established there. Curtiss stayed in Hammondsport with his grandmother to finish primary school. When he graduated from eighth grade in 1892, he moved to Rochester to get a job. He was hired by the Eastman Dry Plate and Film Company, the predecessor organization to Eastman Kodak. While there, he invented another time saving device: a rack to hold the film on which he needed to stencil numbers. This allowed him to stencil 2,500 strips a day when the average for other workers was 250 per day. His boss quickly adopted Curtiss's device for all of the stencilers.

When Kodak opened its new camera factory on State Street in 1893, Curtiss was moved to the new plant. He immediately took to cameras and photography, and it became one of his lifelong passions, but he wasn't enamored of factory work. As soon as he could afford to do so, he purchased a "real" bicycle and went to work for Western Union as a messenger.

Curtiss was infatuated with transportation-related technology from then on. He started making weekend trips down to Hammondsport on his bike (about sixty-five miles each way) and on one of his trips there, he was asked to join the local bicycle racing team called the Hammondsport Boys. His next bike was a Stearns Racer, which he was able to purchase at half price (fifty dollars) because the races he was winning were great advertisement for the manufacturers. When the head of the Hammondsport bicycle group moved to Buffalo, Curtiss took charge.

Curtiss's mother remarried in 1895, and when she became pregnant in 1897, she moved back south to Rock Stream, New York, near Hammondsport. Curtiss returned to live with her and her new husband. On one of his perennial bike rides through the countryside, Curtiss met a young woman who was picking grapes, and on March 7, 1898, he and Lena Perl Neff were married in Hammondsport. They moved in with his grandmother, and Curtiss went to work for a photography studio as a traveling photographer.

But as much as he loved photography, he loved the tinkering with bicycles more, and when a friend of his got out of the bicycle business in 1900, Curtiss replaced him and opened his own bicycle shop on Pulteney Street in Hammondsport. It was in this shop that Curtiss conducted many of his later experiments in transportation. He originally repaired bikes there but thought he could be selling them more cheaply than other manufacturers were, so he contracted with another company to build bikes that he had designed under a brand called Hercules.

On a trip to the Pan-American Exposition that was held in Buffalo in 1901, Curtiss purportedly saw his first motorcycle, the Thomas Auto-Bi, built by the Buffalo-based E.R. Thomas Motor Company, and decided he wanted to try to motorize one of his bicycles. He ordered an engine from the Thomas Company and mounted it to his bicycle. It worked so well that be decided he wanted to try something bigger and faster. His second attempt was with a larger motor, also from Thomas, which weighed in at 180 pounds. From then on, he started building his own engines.

Cyanotype of Curtiss on his bike, circa 1899. *From the author's collection.*

Throughout the early 1900s, Curtiss's exploits were reported in the *Hammondsport Herald* and reprinted in the surrounding area newspapers. One such report in the *Bath Plaindealer* noted, "G.H Curtiss has just returned from a trip to Bergen, N.Y., on one of his Hercules motor cycles. He went by way of Dansville, Mt. Morris, Geneseo and Rochester and returned by Fairport, Palmyra, Canandaigua and Branchport, covering the 200 miles without mishap, at an average speed of twenty miles an hour." Curtiss was an active supporter of the Hammondsport Wheelmen, often donating prizes for races in addition to participating in the festivities.

Curtiss turned to aviation around 1904, when he was contacted about his motorcycle engines by Thomas S. Baldwin, generally referred to as "Captain" Baldwin. Baldwin was a San Francisco innovator who was working with dirigibles (i.e., large, usually torpedo-shaped, gas-inflated balloons). Baldwin purchased engines from Curtiss and installed them on his crafts. The first one was a used engine Curtiss had sent him in 1904, just in time for Baldwin to make history at the Louisiana Purchase Exposition, better known today as the St. Louis World's Fair. His fifty-

Captain Tom Baldwin's dirigible. *Courtesy of the Library of Congress.*

two-foot-long-by-seventeen-feet-wide silk dirigible, the *California Arrow*, which was inflated with hydrogen and powered by the Curtiss engine, was purportedly the first aircraft to successfully fly a circuit in the country. Baldwin's first flight took place in August 1904. On Halloween that same year, the ship won the aerial grand prize at the fair.

A spin-off of the Automobile Club of America called the Aero Club of America was created the following October, and in New York City, in January 1906, the club held its first event in cooperation with the annual Automobile Club Show. Curtiss attended, as he usually did, and there, he met Alexander Graham Bell, who, himself, was trying to develop an aircraft. Bell ordered an engine from Curtiss and had it sent to his vacation home in Nova Scotia, where he was conducting flight experiments using a large kite.

Although he was dabbling in the aviation world, Curtiss retained his interest in motorcycles. In January 1907, after the normal motorcycle races ended in Ormond Beach, Florida, Curtiss brought out his forty-horsepower V-8 engine motorcycle to give it a tryout. He covered the mile track in about twenty-six seconds, which was 136.36 miles per hour. This earned him the title of the "World's Fastest Man," which he held until 1911, when a racecar driver beat his motorcycle's speed.

Back in the aero world, the San Francisco earthquake and fire, which occurred on April 18, 1906, burned down Baldwin's plant and turned three of his four dirigibles to ashes. The fourth, fortunately, had been sent to Curtiss. After the fire, Baldwin decided to move his manufacturing concerns to Hammondsport. Once relocated, Baldwin and Curtiss worked together on the vehicles, but they were still having trouble with them, and Curtiss couldn't figure out what the problem was because Baldwin was doing all the flying. On June 28, 1907, Curtiss piloted the dirigible for the first time. What is interesting to note is that most of the accounts of this flight imply that Baldwin, not Curtiss, was the pilot. The full-page spread, complete with "exclusive" photographs in the *Buffalo Sunday Morning News* does include a photo of Curtiss, but the text of the article itself never mentions him. Not surprisingly, the *Hammondsport Herald* mentions that Curtiss was the pilot and includes a note about his reaction to his first flight: "It is delightful, only there is no place to go." Curtiss's 1907 dirigible flight set a record time and distance aloft, and it was reported in more than a dozen newspapers across the country including those in Chicago, St. Louis, and many smaller towns and villages. Some additional comments from the *Buffalo News* article include:

> *That the dawn of the airship era is at hand was amply demonstrated when, on Thursday of the past week, in the presence of several thousand spectators, including scientific men from the United States War Department and a number of colleges, Captain Thomas Scott Baldwin made a very successful trip in his new dirigible airship, the Twentieth Century...kept the big airship high above the village for a period of about thirty minutes... and bringing it safely to the ground.*

So started another of Curtiss's passions in life. Bell and Curtiss had stayed in touch with one another after they had met in 1906, and in July 1907, Curtiss traveled to Nova Scotia to meet with Bell. It turned out that other aeronautic pioneers were also there, and as they energetically advanced many theories to test, Mrs. Bell urged them to create a research group to decide on the best way forward "to get into the air." The association Curtiss and Bell formed with Casey Baldwin (no relation to Captain Tom), as well as J.A.D. McCurdy and Lieutenant Tom Selfridge, was called the Aerial Experiment Association (AEA). In an interesting side note, the funding for the group was provided by Mrs. Bell, and President Teddy Roosevelt himself approved Lieutenant Selfridge's involvement.

Glenn Curtiss in front of one of his airplanes, circa 1915. *Courtesy of the Library of Congress.*

In November 1907, the Curtiss Manufacturing Company merged with the Baldwin Dirigible Airship Company and the International Aero Vehicle Company, creating the Curtiss Motor Vehicle Company, which was still headquartered in Hammondsport. Surprisingly, Curtiss was vice-president of this new organization, and the president was W.G. Critchlow, who was from the Dayton, Ohio–based International Aero Vehicle Company. The new company continued to build airplane engines and manufacture dirigibles, and it is often credited as being the first true airplane manufacturing company in the country.

The AEA's original plan was to motorize one of Bell's kites, known as the Cygnet Tetrahedral Kite, and get it flying, but an early attempt at a manned flight of the kite demolished it, so the association turned to gliders instead. The group constructed a series of "aerodromes," the early name for airplanes, which were referred to by their numbers. Drome #1 was constructed in Hammondsport and nicknamed *Red Wing* because its wings were covered with red silk. On March 12, 1908, Casey Baldwin took off in the "aerodrome," and because all of the Wright brother's flights were done in secret, this marked the first public airplane flight in the country. As noted in the *Washington, D.C. Evening Star* the following day:

> *The aeroplane Redwing* [sic]*, in its first trial here yesterday, made the first public flight of a "heavier than air" machine in America, covering a distance of 319 feet at a speed of 30 miles an hour.... The machine...rose*

to a height varying from ten to twenty feet. It had perfect stability, and the flight might have continued indefinitely had it not been for the breaking of one of the supports in the rear surface, causing the machine to swing to the right and come to the ice.

The association's next vehicle was called the *White Wing* because, rather than silk, its wing covering was made of white muslin. This plane also had what was then a novel feature: wheels. On his thirtieth birthday (May 21, 1908), Curtiss flew drome #2 over 339 yards. From the *Boston Globe*, we learned:

G.H. Curtiss made a flight of 339 yards in Baldwin's "White Wing."… The machine was under perfect control at all times and was steered first to the right and then to the left before landing. The 339 yards was covered in 19 seconds, or 37 miles per hour.…The motor is a duplicate of the one used by Curtiss when he made his record of a mile in 26.2–5 seconds, or at a rate of 136.4 miles per hour.

Drome #3's nickname broke the color pattern of names with Bell's name of *June Bug*. Curtiss was the project manager on this build, and he hoped to make it fly both faster and more accurately. Less than two months after his *White Wing* flight, on Independence Day in 1908, Curtiss flew the *June Bug* at nearly forty miles an hour for more than a mile. A film of the flight was shown in theaters nationwide. This plane was forty feet wide, twenty-eight feet long and used the same forty-horsepower motor as the *White Wing*. It had been tested for several weeks prior to the event, and those tests had also been heavily reported. The Independence Day flight was reported the next day in the *Rochester Democrat and Chronicle*:

Glenn H. Curtiss, of Hammondsport, to-day [sic] *successfully contested for the silver cup offered several months ago by the Scientific American for the longest flight made by an heavier-than-air flying machine. The flight was made by the flying machine June Bug, a type of aeroplane upon which Mr. Curtiss, in company with Professor Alexander Graham Bell, has for the past year been engaged.*

Mr. Curtiss operated the machine himself. His first flight lacked a foot of the distance prescribed by the rules of the contest, 3,690 feet, but the second flight covered over a mile, which he traveled in a minute and a fraction.

Unfortunately, all the attention that Curtiss and the AEA received from that *June Bug* flight annoyed the Wright brothers, and they started a decades-long patent war against Curtiss, claiming they had the rights to *all* airplane flight control technology. Even though their planes used flexible wings and Curtiss's used rigid wings with flaps (called ailerons), the brothers insisted that their patent #821393—for which they filed on March 23, 1903, but which was not granted until 1906 and was for gliders, not motorized vehicles—covered Curtiss's motorized planes. The first legal action against Curtiss was heard in Buffalo in January 1910. There, Judge John R. Hazel agreed with the Wrights and placed an injunction against Curtiss. In June that same year, the U.S. Circuit Court of Appeals reversed Hazel's decision. In February 1913, Hazel ruled again in favor of the plaintiffs, but Curtiss was still able to keep producing planes. The battles continued until World War I, when the military stepped in and told both firms to let it go and focus on developing the war planes the troops needed.

While the patent wars raged with the Wrights, Curtiss continued to develop, build and sell airplanes. His first sale was also the first in the country to a non-military buyer; it was sold to the New York Aeronautical Society. In 1909, Curtiss won the Gordon Bennett Race in Rheims, France, earning him a purse of $15,000 and prompting the *New York Times* profile mentioned earlier. In fact, that Sunday issue contained seven articles on Curtiss, including the full-page spread. With his win in France, the paper proclaimed Curtiss the "King of the Air."

The year 1909 continued to be a good one for Curtiss. He participated in another event that earned him the second notch in his belt on his way to the *Scientific American* trophy, and the following May, he won the third *Scientific American* race, yielding another $10,000 in prizes. The cup was a silver one that was designed by Tiffany's.

With that accomplishment behind him, Curtiss turned to a different kind of plane design: seaboats and amphibian planes. He spent much of 1911 designing boats that could fly and planes with pontoons that could fly and function on the water. He designed planes that could do both, and he also proved to the U.S. Navy that it was possible to take off from and land on a ship.

At the start of World War I, in 1914, the British were quick to recognize that having an air force could help them greatly in quickly winning the war. They turned to the Curtiss Aeroplane Company to build 250 planes, but the Hammondsport factory space was not large enough to produce that many planes that quickly. Even with a workforce of nearly two hundred people working twenty-four hours a day, they were running behind schedule. The other challenge was the shipping of the completed planes. As noted in the December 14, 1914 edition of the *Elmira Star-Gazette*, the planes were being sent via the Lackawanna Railroad to New York City, where they were shipped, at least in this case, via the *Lusitania* to England. Both of these factors troubled Curtiss, and he was looking for a larger facility with better transportation options. There were rumors that Curtiss was going to move his manufacturing to France to get out of the patent wars with the Wrights, but on December 5, 1914, the Buffalo papers broke the news that Curtiss was moving his operations to Buffalo. Ironically, the building he was going to occupy belonged to the former E.R. Thomas Company from which he had ordered his first motor. Although Curtiss moved the airplane factory to Buffalo, his original motor factory stayed in Hammondsport.

Unfortunately for Curtiss, the Wrights were not the only people challenging Curtiss on patent infringement. In 1915, he was involved in another suit, this one with Albert Janin about Curtiss's use of his "flying boats," noted above, and the predecessor to the seaplanes of today. In a *Hammondsport Herald* article from February of that year titled "Glenn Curtiss Explains the Janin Patent," we learn the following:

> *The dispute between Curtiss and Janin has been very generally taken to refer to basic patents on the flying boat. The patents really involved are on a device balancing the flying machine in the water and helping it to rise from the surface of the water under high speed. The device consists of two floats, one under the outer end of each lower wing, and the patent particularly relates to a very small wooden plane attached to the bottom of each of these floats. In his statement, Mr. Curtiss says: "Mr. Janin and his attorney are quite premature in announcing the award of the invention of the hydro-aeroplane of Mr. Janin. The Janin claim does not involve the features which made the hydro-aeroplane a successful flying machine or the features of the flying boat. The decision in question is but a preliminary one.... When this final decision is given, and not until then, will any statements of Mr. Janin's concerning the award of the invention be entitled to serious consideration.*

While these patent fights continued, so did World War I. Everyone had thought that the war would be over quickly, but as it dragged on, more equipment was needed. A year after Curtiss's company moved to Buffalo, it won another contract with the British, this one for $15 million. By 1917,

Postcard of Curtiss Manufacturing. *From the author's collection.*

it was clear that even the new plant was too small, so plans were drawn to construct a new $4 million, seventy-two-acre factory on Elmwood Avenue. Construction started in July 1917 and was completed in October. When it opened, the new plant employed eighteen thousand people.

The Curtiss manufacturing complexes were located north of downtown Buffalo, but the airport used for testing the planes was located in the eastern suburb of Cheektowaga, where the current Buffalo Niagara International Airport is located. It was also during this time that Curtiss created a research arm in Garden City, New York, called the Curtiss Engineering Corporation. The research being conducted by this new company was where Curtiss's heart was, so he left the manufacturing business to run research and development.

Curtiss was not the only one making news from his inventions. On June 20, 1917, Katherine Stinson flew a Curtiss "Jenny" plane from Curtiss Field in Buffalo to a variety of other cities on her way to Washington, D.C., to deliver funds that had been collected for the Red Cross. Stinson was purported to be only nineteen at the time, and she was already a seasoned pilot who had earned her pilot's license in 1912, when she was merely twelve years old. However, the newspaper accounts were not correct; she was born in 1891 and was twenty-one when she got her license and twenty-six by 1917. Still, she was only the fourth women to earn a license.

Katherine Stinson and her Curtiss plane, circa 1917. *Courtesy of the Library of Congress.*

Not content with just one specialty, Curtiss started to combine his love of aviation with his love of ground travel in 1917. In the spring of that year, the company introduced a novelty vehicle known as the autoplane. As the name implies, the machine could fly in the air and drive on land. It had a thirty-gallon fuel tank and could travel on that amount of fuel for approximately three hours. A profile of the autoplane appeared in several journals of that era, including the March 24, 1917 issue of the *Scientific American*.

When the armistice was signed on November 11, 1918, World War I was finally over, and the various military units canceled an estimated $75 million in contracts with Curtiss. The large new factory building was empty and was later sold, as was the original Hammondsport Manufacturing Facility. The company consolidated its work to the Garden City location. More than a decade later, on June 26, 1929, most of the patent battles finally ended with the merger of the Curtis Aeroplane and Motor Corporation with the Wright Aeronautical Corporation and eight other aerospace firms, including six Curtiss subsidiaries. The resulting company was named Curtiss-Wright Corporation and became headquartered near Buffalo in a new facility in Tonawanda.

Glenn Curtiss moved to Florida after World War I and became a real estate mogul, developing the cities around Miami, including Opa-Locka, Miami Springs and Hialeah. He also continued inventing things, including the aero car, a travel trailer shaped much like today's Airstream trailers that used a fifth wheel hitch, also of his design. He had also started to design an aero car that was self-propelled, like today's recreational vehicles (RVs). A smaller trailer, which he called the "motorbungalo," was the predecessor to today's pop-up tent trailers, and to get around in the Everglades, he invented what is now called an air boat, a jet-engine propelled fan boat he called the scooter.

Although the lawsuits with the Wrights and their heirs ended with the 1929 corporate merger, in June 1930, Curtiss faced a settlement hearing launched by the heirs of August Herring, who had been his partner in the Curtiss-Herring Corporation that the two had founded. Curtiss was traveling to the Rochester court to testify when he felt an intense pain; this turned out to be acute appendicitis. He was sent to Buffalo General Hospital for surgery, which went well. He had missed the court appearance, though, and the Herring attorney speculated that he was faking an illness. He was not, and it turned out to be worse than anyone expected. In the early morning hours of July 23, 1930, while still in the hospital recovering

Elevation of the autoplane, showing the staggered planes, propeller and tail features

Left: Curtiss's auto-plane. *Courtesy of the* Scientific American, *March 24, 1917.*

Below: Curtiss flying boats in the factory. *Courtesy of the* NY Tribune, *August 5, 1917.*

from the operation, Curtiss died from a pulmonary embolism on the way to the bathroom. He was found on the floor by his nurse.

Despite Curtiss's death, Curtiss-Wright continued to produce military airplanes throughout the 1930s and until the end of World War II. Its primary airplane was the P-40, which was first tested at the corporate test field in Cheektowaga in 1938. In 1940, the factory in Tonawanda had more than five thousand workers and it was still growing. An additional facility was opened in 1941 on Genesee Street, and it added a new research building nearby in 1943. By that time, Curtiss-Wright employed more than forty-three thousand people. In total, its factories built nearly seventeen thousand planes during World War II. Most of those planes, about fourteen thousand, were P-40s.

At the end of the war, the company had been reduced to about 5,500 employees, but it was not able to develop a solid non-military clientele, so in 1946, Curtiss-Wright ceased production in the Buffalo area plants. Plant 1 in Tonawanda was taken over by Western Electric, whereas Plant 2 became a Westinghouse facility. The aircraft research building was donated to Cornell University, which renamed it the Cornell Aeronautical Laboratories. This went on to be renamed Calspan in 1972.

When Glenn Curtiss died, he was only fifty-two years old. From his first refinement of a sled to his travel trailers, Curtiss purportedly invented more than five hundred things. This is difficult to verify, however. Unlike some of the other inventors discussed here, Curtiss did not apply for patents on most of these. He felt, as Dart did, that inventions belonged to those who needed them to build new inventions. But even if the numbers are exaggerated, there is no doubt that Curtiss was an innovator and a shrewd businessman who turned a series of improved machines into a billion-dollar business, improving all of our lives along the way.

8.

JOHN OISHEI AND WINDSHIELD WIPERS

In 1916, John Oishei was involved in a traffic accident that led to his business producing automobile windshield wipers. The local myth is that Oishei was the first inventor of the devices, but, in fact, Mary Anderson patented them more than ten years earlier, in 1903. This chapter describes how the myth developed and, more importantly, the Buffalo business Oishei established, remnants of which still fund many of the area's charities.

John Roffo Oishei was born on January 18, 1886, to Charles Humbert Oishei and Julia Ruth Roffo. It appears that Oishei's paternal grandfather, Giuseppe, immigrated from Italy to the southern United States, arriving first in New Orleans, then moving to Memphis, where Oishei's father, Charles, was born. Eventually, the family headed north, to Buffalo, New York. John Roffo, Oishei's maternal grandfather, is credited by some as the first Italian resident of Buffalo, arriving in 1845.

Both sides of the Oishei family were staunchly Catholic. Oishei's mother was a soprano soloist at St. Joseph's Cathedral, as well as the organist for the May evening devotions. She also performed for the Irish National League meetings. His parents' wedding announcement in the local newspapers named his father as Achille, although Achille was his father, Charles's, brother. Julia and Charles were married on February 11, 1885, in St. Joseph's Cathedral in downtown Buffalo. Charles worked in a variety of jobs to support the family, and then in 1890, he received his law degree from the relatively new Buffalo Law School, the predecessor of the UB School of Law.

It was not uncommon at this time to have large families, and John Oishei (note that his name is sometimes spelled as Oshei or, rarely, O'shei) was the oldest child in a family with eight children. The family lived on Maryland Street, which was in an Italian enclave on the west side of Buffalo. Oishei's mother died in 1904, when John was eighteen and his youngest sibling was only four, so, as was often the case in that era, he did not continue on with school, as he had to help with his younger siblings still at home. When his father remarried, he gained three stepsiblings.

Perhaps because of a love of music Oishei inherited from his mother, one of his early jobs was at the Star Theater in Buffalo, which occupied the triangular corner of Genesee, Mohawk and Pearl Streets. In addition to the Star, Buffalo had several theaters at that time, including the Academy, Garden, Lafayette and Teck Theaters. While at the Star, Oishei gained a reputation for being an affable and confident fellow, and he was well liked by the patrons, including some of Buffalo's wealthier citizens. He was promoted from usher through a series of other positions and finally became the manager.

When Oishei turned twenty-one in 1907, he embarked on a relocation treadmill. In February of that year, Oishei left the Star Theater for the Greenwall Theater in New Orleans, but he was only there until May, when he returned to operate the Shuberts' Teck Theater in Buffalo; the Shuberts also owned the New Orleans Greenwall, where he had spent the previous three months. He left Buffalo again in August 1907, this time to manage the Shuberts' Kansas City theater, and he returned to the Teck in September to turn the theater into a successful vaudeville house. Oishei continued to work at the Buffalo Teck Theater until August 1924, well after he'd started his other various businesses.

According to the records in the New York State Marriage Index and an announcement in the *Buffalo Enquirer*, Oishei married Estelle Reed Low(e) on April 21, 1908—not in 1911, as some sources suggest. Low and her family had moved from Pennsylvania to Buffalo in 1902 so that her father could work on the Buffalo Harbor break wall. Their eldest son, John Reed Oishei, was born in January 1910. The couple had three children in total: John, Julian and Patricia. Estelle died in 1938, when she was fifty-four and Oishei was fifty-two, and he never remarried.

Oishei was constantly thinking of ways to improve his hometown. In 1911, he proposed a plan to revise the route of the Elmwood and Hoyt Trolley Car Lines to take people more effectively to and from the theater district of downtown. A map of the plan was published in the September

John R. Oishei. *From the John R. Oishei Foundation collection.*

2 edition of the *Buffalo Evening News*, and it proposed a loop on Elmwood Street and the supporting side streets, with two cars running the loop. The plan was supported by Ansley Wilcox, Edward Hengerer and several other members of the Buffalo Retail Merchants Association. So, Oishei was clearly thinking of transportation issues at least five years before his passion turned to windshield wipers.

Proceeding Oishei's 1916 inspiration, there were several other windshield wiper inventors. The first was Robert Douglas, who filed for his patent on wipers in March 1903. His patent was for locomotive windshields, and no one saw the crossover market for automobiles. He was followed closely by Mary Anderson from Birmingham, Alabama. Her inspiration came during a trip out of town to New York City during a snowstorm. She noticed that the snow was piling up on the windshield of the trolley she was riding in and blocking the driver's vision; he even had to put his head out the window to see. She sketched her wipers while still on the trolley and was granted patent #743801 on November 10, 1903. She contacted manufacturers to try to develop her wipers but was unsuccessful. Although she did find a company to produce them, she was unable to sell them because they were designed

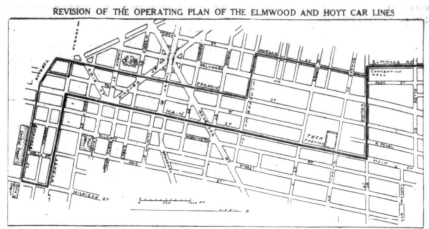

REVISION OF THE OPERATING PLAN OF THE ELMWOOD AND HOYT CAR LINES

Proposed by J. R. Oishei, and approved of by Ansley Wilcox, G. B. Mann, C. Theo. Seven, George W. Benton, Charles C. Boache, Edward L. Hengerer, T. M. Gibson and other members of the Retail Merchants' Association.

Oishei's plan for trolleys. *Courtesy of the* Buffalo Evening News, *September 2, 1911.*

for trolleys, and there weren't many cars yet. There was also some concern that the wipers would actually make it more difficult to see, not easier. Her patent expired in 1920.

Cars in this era were not just a U.S. phenomenon, and the need for windshield wipers was international. British inventor James Henry Apjohn also filed a patent application in 1903, his in the UK. While these wipers were designed to be manually operated, U.S. designer Charlotte Bridgwood, in 1913, invented the first automatic wipers. Her patent was granted in 1917, and her wipers were manufactured and sold as "electric storm windshield wipers."

In 1913, Oishei and ten other investors, including Michael Shea and Peter Cornell, became part owners in the Whitmier-Ferris Company, a billboard advertising company. Oishei was the treasurer of the company, and his experience in this business helped him immensely when he transitioned to marketing his windshield wipers.

It is important to note that, during this time, Buffalo was deeply steeped in the auto industry. Pierce-Arrow and the E.R. Thomas Motor Company were started and headquartered in Buffalo, and Ford and General Motors also had plants in the city. The Thomas Flyer won the New York to Paris automobile race in 1908. Although the Thomas Motor Company closed and sold its plant to Glenn Curtiss in late 1914, the city was still considered among the pioneer automobile cities.

As the legend goes, Oishei turned to notions of manufacturing windshield wipers in 1916, when he had a car accident in the rain. He was driving down Delaware Avenue, Buffalo's noted Millionaires' Row, in his National Roadster when he hit a person on a bicycle whom he had not seen because of the rain on the windshield. Although the rider was, thankfully, unharmed, it profoundly affected Oishei, and he became driven to solve the problem. He tried several different approaches, but none worked, and then, serendipity struck again. While shopping in a Buffalo store, Oishei saw something that would work: a hand drawn squeegee being sold by an inventor named John W. Jepson. (Note that several sources say that Oishei's fateful accident happened in 1917, but the wipers were already being sold in 1916.)

Oishei decided to locate Jepson, and when he found him, he offered to help him market his invention. With the financial backing of several of his wealthy theater patrons, such as Peter Cornell and William Haines, Oishei started a company to market Rain Rubber, as the wipers were dubbed. This 1916 incarnation of the company held offices in the Sidway Building, which had been on the corner of Main Street and Goodell Street. The wipers were manufactured by eight employees in a building at 2665 Main Street. Oishei wasted no time in getting the wipers on the market. In 1916 and 1917, he attended the National Exhibition for Ford Accessories to demonstrate them and started a fierce marketing campaign.

By 1920, he had used his contacts and advertising experience to get advertisements and product announcements in more than two dozen trade journals, including the *American Cooperative Journal* (1916), *Automobile Trade Directory*, *Automobile Trade Journal*, *Automobile Journal*, *Chilton Automobile Directory*, the *Commercial Car Journal*, *India Rubber World*, *Accessory and Garage Journal*, *Texas Trade Review and Industrial Record*, *Automobile Topics*, *Hardware Dealers Magazine*, *Scientific American*, the *Horseless Age*, *Motor West*, the *American Exporter*, *American Garage and Auto Dealer*, *Motor World*, *Motor Record*, *Electric Vehicles*, the *Fordowner*, the *Rubber Age*, *Automobile Dealer and Repairer* and *Rubber World*. It's important to note that two of these were international journals.

So, how did this windshield wiper work, and why was it so popular? A September 1917 new product announcement in the *Rubber Age and Tire News* explained:

> In mounting upon the windshield, a device to clear rain from it and thus ensure clear vision in a storm, many owners prefer one that may be quickly removed when it is not needed, as in clear weather. Although acknowledging that a strip of rubber drawn across wet glass will wipe all water from the glass surface, many drivers want to keep their shields free from attachments. To meet such preferences, the Universal Rain Rubber is designed to be

quickly and easily attached to or removed from a two-piece shield. It consists primarily of a traveling section, which is mounted in and slides along the opening between the upper and lower halves of the windshield, holding on to the edge of the glass as a channel. Two arms project from this section, one to each panel of the shield, and on each arm are two strips of rubber set edgewise, so that when moved across the glass, water is pressed off by the close fit of the rubber on glass. Rivets holding the various parts together are topped with celluloid to prevent scratching. Adjustments permit the moving from normal of the glass halves of the windshield. In five models to fit practically any type of two-piece windshield, the Universal is manufactured by the Tri-Continental Corp., Buffalo, N.Y.

A Rubber Windshield Clearer

The Universal Rain Rubber, designed to clear any type of two-piece windshield, is being offered by the Tri-Continental Co., Sidway Bldg., Buffalo, N. Y. This device clears

The Universal Rain Rubber
A device for clearing a two-piece windshield, snow, etc.

both the top and bottom glass straight across, a unique feature being a traveling section which slides on the slot.

It can be quickly attached and holds firmly in place. It is made of two pieces of gum rubber with two cleaning surfaces on each arm. The rivets have celluloid heads that prevent the glass from being scratched. The device can be removed by simply opening the glass and lifting the Rain Rubber off. It is made in five models and sells for $1.50 in the United States.

Description of the universal rain rubber. *Courtesy of the* Automobile Trade Journal, *Volume 22, 1917.*

Most of the advertisements and product announcements contained similar text and were accompanied by a wide variety of illustrations. The four-panel illustration that accompanied this advertisement was one of the more elaborate ones. Although this particular advertisement did not include a price, others did. The devices sold for $1.50 each.

At some point during World War I, Trico switched from its normal operations to producing parts for ammunition boxes for the war effort. It manufactured the boxes' locks and hinges. Still, by 1918, the Tri-Continental Corporation had sold enough wipers for Oishei to buy out John Jepson's shares in the company, but the real breakthrough for the company came in 1919, when the Buffalo-based Pierce-Arrow Motor Car Company used the wiper as standard equipment on its cars. The other luxury cars of the era, Packard, Cadillac and Lincoln followed suit the next year, and the Tri-Continental Corporation was on its way.

During this era, across the country, there was a variety of labor-related unrest. Workers were organizing in unions in an effort to win higher wages and a shorter work week. The

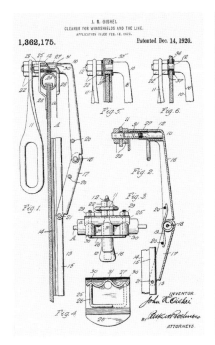

Left: Oishei patent. *Courtesy of the United States Patent and Trademark Office.*

Right: Windshield washer advertisement. *Courtesy of* Motor Age, *1948.*

Tri-Continental Corporation was an early adopter of the new standards, announcing in 1919 that it had switched to a forty-eight-hour work week and that it was paying workers eighty cents per hour. Similar companies in the Buffalo area were paying between seventy and seventy-five cents per hour. Trico continued to expand, and in 1920, it moved its manufacturing operations into an 1890 building that was previously used for cold storage by the Christian Weyand Brewery before it closed due to Prohibition. The building at 624 Ellicott Street became known as Trico Plant 1.

On February 18, 1920, Oishei submitted a patent application for his wiper system called the "Cleaner for Windshields and the Like." To prepare for expansion into the international market, which the company believed that invention would stir, Trico Products Corporation (Trico) was incorporated on April 26, 1920, and it took over all the operations of the previous Tri-Continental Corporation. The new patent, #1362175, was granted ten months after its filing, on December 14, 1920.

With this new patent in hand, Trico opened an office in Detroit to try to get windshield wipers installed as standard equipment on all cars, not just the luxury cars they were already on. The plan was successful, and Ford began including the Rain Rubber on all new models.

As Buffalo and the country moved into the 1920s, people continued to move to urban areas. Buffalo's population had grown to more than 500,000 and the nation's population topped 100 million, despite the devastation caused by the 1918 influenza pandemic. It is estimated that the total wealth in the country almost doubled in this decade. People were not just buying automobiles but a variety of new technological innovations powered by electricity. Radios were making their way into homes, as well. After Prohibition ended, the "Roaring Twenties" went into full swing.

The nationwide vehicle production topped four million a year (cars and trucks) in 1923, and Trico had a lock on the windshield wiper market by that time. It had also moved into the automatic windshield wiper market by purchasing a Cleveland company that had been founded by William Folberth. Folberth had developed his wipers in 1920 and received his subsequent patent on them in 1922 (#1420538). These original automatic wipers had a severe limitation, however. They only worked when the car was moving. Trico had also developed an automatic wiper system in 1920 but purchased Folberth's company to minimize competition and avoid and settle patent lawsuits. The new automatic wipers retailed for $3.29.

In 1924, there was an explosion at Plant 1 that damaged the plant and leveled several nearby buildings. In July that year, the company filed for permits to build a new $7,000 "steel-and-asbestos" building at that site. The plant was enlarged for $4,000 in 1925. The company was always people-oriented and supported the employment of disabled people, hiring blind workmen as early as 1925.

Toward the end of the 1920s, Trico continued to innovate the wiper market, and in 1927, their new stock offering was published in the *Hartford Courant, Pittsburgh Post-Gazette, Boston Globe, Scranton Republican, D&C, Burlington Free Press* and the *Cincinnati Enquirer*. In 1928, advertisements for the stocks on the market included promotions of the new rear-view mirrors called, at the time, "rear-vision" mirrors. In February 1929, they purchased two lots (in total, 140 feet long) on Washington Street for additional space. That same year, they started producing the first dual-wiper system. In April, their stock increased dramatically on the news of a five-year contract with GM, and in October, it was producing twenty thousand units of wipers a day. Prior to the stock market crash on October 24, 1929, shares were selling at about sixty dollars each. After the crash, they were down to thirty dollars.

Although the company is primarily remembered for its flagship windshield wipers, Trico sold a variety of automobile accessories. Despite the Great Depression, many of these accessories were created and sold in the 1930s. They included springs, a wooden wheel spoke tightener, throttle guards, coil guards and horns. In 1936, the company introduced the first windshield-washer system, which was advertised with the slogan "two little squirts." It also experimented with an automatic window mechanism called the Lift-O-Matic, which was finally released in 1940. Volume 74 of *Financial World* noted that:

> *The new self-opening windows featured on several 1941 automobile models were designed by Trico Products—called the "Lift-O-Matic," the invention is hailed as eliminating the last semblance of "hand-cranking" from the modern car.*

As the world moved into World War II, Trico again switched from its normal operations to manufacturing munitions. A small announcement with graphic in February 1942 noted that the company had started producing bullet heads for the navy. A special article on women in the workforce in the Lincoln, California *News Messenger* on July 2, 1942 noted:

> *Trico Products corporation, formerly a manufacturer of windshield wipers, is turning to defense work and employing more than 50 percent women, Mrs. Lena H. Cooling, personnel director, said. "This isn't a new policy, for we have always employed more women than men," she added. "The tiny parts used in windshield-wiper assembling necessitated nimble and sensitive fingers."*

The company also helped the war-torn workforce by manufacturing a device to inspect products that could be used by blind workers.

When the war ended, the company's rate of production continued near wartime levels for a number of years. Because windshields were becoming curved, in 1948, Trico introduced the rainbow wiper system, which had a three-part arm to follow that curve. It combined wipers and washers into a single system the following year. In 1950, Trico had about 4,500 employees, but it could not sustain those levels. In July 1952, Trico laid off 2,200 workers. This may have been related to the steel strike that was taking place that had caused the layoffs of more than 60,000 automobile workers.

But the company continued to be one of the most successful local companies in Buffalo, and Oishei was grateful to the city and his workers. As part of the company's diamond anniversary in 1967, Oishei created the John R. Oishei Charitable Appreciation Trust with around eighty-one thousand shares of stock worth more than $10 million. The intent of the trust was to help Trico employees—both past and current—with anything they might need, such as education funding, medical care or other assistance. This was consistent with Oishei's other pro-employee policies, such as providing annual bonuses, life insurance, a pension plan, sick time and disability benefits.

In January 1968, it was announced that Oishei was to retire in the summer and that his son (who used the spelling Oshei for his last name) would be taking over the company. However, Oishei died in his home less than a month later, on January 27, 1968. It is purported that, during his lifetime, Oishei was courted by both General Motors and Ford, but he turned them down out of loyalty to his hometown. Oishei was successful in staying in Buffalo, but after his death, the manufacturing was moved to Texas, where workers earned about one-fourth the amount of Buffalo workers, and Mexico, where workers earned less than one-tenth the amount of Buffalo workers. The company was sold in 1994, and in the early 2000s, the Buffalo plants were permanently closed. By that time, Plant I had grown to a seven-story, six-hundred-thousand-square-foot facility, which is now listed in the National Register of Historic Places.

But despite his death and the closing of his company, Oishei continued to support Buffalo. What had started as around $10 million in 1967 had grown to more than $50 million in 1999, and in 2003, when combined with a foundation that had also been formed by Oishei in 1940, the Julia R. and Estelle L. Foundation, its assets were nearly $250 million. In 2012, the John R. Oishei Foundation donated $10 million to Children's Hospital, which is now called the John R. Oishei Children's Hospital in his honor.

The fact that Oishei's success was based on the inventions of others does not make him any less innovative. Just as Joseph Dart combined steam engines and grain conveyors and funded the construction of the first grain elevators, Oishei combined Jepson's work, his Buffalo contacts and his desire to make cars safer into an international company with a legacy that is still keeping cars safe and making everyone's lives better. It was one of the city's largest private employers, and the foundation it spawned is now one of the city's largest philanthropic organizations.

9.

ALEX OSBORN AND BRAINSTORMING

A lex Osborn was an advertising executive and professor looking for a way to encourage creativity. This chapter describes why Osborn felt there was a need for a more creative thinking process, the controversy around the use of the process and the impact his foundation, now known as the International Center for Studies in Creativity, has had on businesses.

Born on May 24, 1888, in the Bronx, New York, Alexander Faickney Osborn was rarely called by his full name; rather, he preferred to go by Alex or, simply, his initials, A.F.O. His father, John Osborn, was an accountant who married Katherine Lamb in 1875. Alex Osborn was the third of four children, all boys: William, Donald, Alex and Kenneth. According to the 1900 census, William was already working as a lawyer, and the other boys were still in school.

In his early years, Osborn attended Morris High School in the Bronx. In 1905, he began his studies at Hamilton College in Clinton, New York, graduating in 1909. While at Hamilton, Osborn cofounded the college's drama club with Alexander Wolcott, who also went on to be a noted author. In college, he gained a reputation for clowning around, as his ten-year class reunion photo shows. And a fellow graduate, fifty years later, referred to him as one of two "city-slickers" in the class of 1909.

After graduation, Osborn moved to Buffalo and very briefly worked a variety of journalism jobs at the *Buffalo Times* and *Buffalo Express*. From there, he went to work for the Buffalo Chamber of Commerce as the assistant secretary on the publicity committee. He worked there for two years, and for his last

Osborn, on the right with his tongue out, at a ten-year college reunion. *From the Hamilton College collection.*

year, he edited its monthly magazine, the *Live Wire*. During that time, he also represented the chamber, speaking in favor of the new bridge project connecting Buffalo to Fort Erie, Canada, dubbed the Peace Bridge. He did other speeches, highlighting the benefits of Buffalo to businesses. In a speech reported in the *Buffalo Daily Times* on November 26, 1911, he noted:

> *Buffalo has always been six-cylindered. First, there's location: 50,000,000 people within 500 miles. Second, there's transportation; 29 water and rail lines. Third, there's the raw material, all kinds of it within economic reach. Fourth, is labor. There are 75,000 diversified workmen. Fifth, there is natural gas, and sixth, is the power from Niagara, and what is more, this six-cylindered Buffalo has a roomy tonneau of many fair-priced industrial properties where misplaced manufacturers can ride in ease to success.*

The article goes on to say that the speech was well received by the audience, a group of businessmen attending the city's Industrial Week festivities.

As early as 1911, Obsorn was giving talks about his advertising techniques to various Buffalo organizations, such as the YMCA and Teacher's Educational League, as well as graduation events and conferences in Buffalo, Rochester and other cities and chambers of commerce. Also that year, he designed advertising cards that were to be placed on trolleys and other forms of transportation to sell similar benefits of operating businesses in Buffalo.

In January 1912, Osborn resigned from his position at the chamber and went to the Hard Manufacturing Company, a bed manufacturer that is still in business today, as "chief traveling salesman," the equivalent of today's sales manager. By 1913, he was the advertising manager there, and he was also teaching courses on advertising at the YMCA. One of the recurring stories about his position at Hard Manufacturing is that he secured one of the company's beds to a flatbed truck and then drove around the city as a "life-size advertisement."

During this time, he was a member of the local advertising men's club, which met at the Lafayette Hotel. In 1914, he joined the publicity committee for the centenary celebration of the end of the War of 1812, and he moved directly into advertising with a position at the Buffalo-based E.P. Remington Firm. Originally founded by Edward P. Remington in Pittsburgh, the agency was moved to Buffalo in 1913, when Remington died.

It was during these early years in Buffalo that Osborn met Helen Coatsworth, the daughter of lawyer Edward Emerson Coatsworth, who was, at one time, the district attorney for Erie County. The Coatsworths were descendants of a large contingent of family members who immigrated to the United States from Canada in the early 1800s. Helen Coatsworth was a graduate of Buffalo Seminary and was active in the alumni association. On September 5, 1916, at Bay Beach in Ontario, Canada, the couple was married. The couple was living in Canada when they were wed, perhaps at the Coatsworth summer home, and then, they moved to 78 Inwood Place in Buffalo.

While Osborn worked at Remington, he lived at the Buffalo YMCA and was the editor of the local *Y Magazine*. During World War I, the publisher of that *Y Magazine* knew Bruce Barton and suggested that the two men team up on the YMCA's United War Work campaign. They did, working out of Washington, D.C., and a short time later, they added a third member, Roy S. Durstine, who was a former reporter for the *NY Sun* and a partner of a small advertising agency called Berrien & Durstine. They raised more than $200 million (nearly $3.5 billion today) for the "Seven Sobbing Sisters": the YMCA, YWCA, Salvation Army, National Catholic War Council, Jewish Welfare Board, War Camp Community Service and the American Library Association.

Osborn was also actively involved in raising money for the four phases of the Liberty Loan Campaigns, which likely helped lead to his post at the YMCA. He remained active in this position while working on the War Work Campaign, and in a 1918 Buffalo celebration of the success of the promotions, he was honored by introducing the famous actor Douglas Fairbanks as the celebrity guest.

As legend has it, the impetus behind what would become the world-famous BBDO advertising agency came when Osborn and Barton were having lunch at Grand Central Station's Oyster Bar after the war ended. While musing on what to do with their futures, Osborn suggested Barton start an advertising business. Barton said he would enjoy the creative aspects but didn't like the business side (hiring, firing and finances), so Osborn suggested that he bring in Durstine as business manager. Barton agreed to give it a shot and borrowed $10,000 to start his own business with Durstine, and they opened Barton and Durstine on January 2, 1919.

Seven months later, the pair asked Osborn to join them, which he did with the condition that he be allowed to stay primarily in Buffalo. The company's name was changed to Barton, Durstine and Osborn. Osborn was already well known in the Buffalo market. In addition to the mattress ploy mentioned earlier, he had run a contest for General Baking Co. for women baking their own bread. Osborn was concerned that the contest would be a bust and was amazed when more than one thousand women participated.

Osborn was a member of many clubs, including the local Rotary Club. He was quoted in the *Buffalo Times* on February 23, 1920:

> *Rotary never side-steps a responsibility or "passes the buck" to the other fellow. To the Rotarian, life is an investment that must yield dividends that are better than dollars, and that are not measured in terms of commerce. To the Rotarian, community prosperity is more important than personal profit. He never "knocks" a good thing, nor praises a bad thing. His city is the best in the country, and his country the best in the world. He works hard, plays square, and gives with a smile.*

These were not just words to Osborn. His devotion to all in his life would prove that he lived by these sentiments, both personally and professionally.

And on that professional side, in 1928, Osborn's firm merged with George Batten Co., another leading firm founded in 1891. The new company name was Batten, Barton, Durstine & Osborn (BBDO), a now legendary advertising agency. BBDO clients included heavy manufacturing giants General Electric, General Motors, U.S. Steel, Dunlop Tire and B.F. Goodrich, but also Lever Brothers and Betty Crocker. In fact, although she has been modernized over the years, it was BBDO who created the iconic image of Betty Crocker we know today. Osborn served as the executive vice-president from 1939 to 1945 and as the chairman and vice-chairman before

Osborn portrait. *From the Hamilton College collection.*

retiring in 1960. The firm went on to have offices in fifty-two countries and multimillion-dollar accounts.

According to his obituary and other sources, Osborn first started thinking about the importance of ideas and imagination when applying for a new job after he was fired as a cub reporter. The new editor purportedly told him, "Your writing is amateurish, but I'm going to give you a trial because each piece seems to have an idea." He said it started his obsession with developing at least one good idea every day.

Although BBDO was an iconic advertising agency, most of what we know about Osborn comes from his prolific writing about ideation. His first two known publications were before BBDO: a missive titled *Brass Tacks of Advertising* was printed in 1915 by the Buffalo-based Hausauer-Jones Printing Company, and his next publication was *The Optimism Book for Offices*, which was published by Art Metal Construction Company in 1918 in Jamestown, New York. As his second publication's title implies, it was an instruction book on how to get business offices functioning again after the end of the War to End All Wars (World War I).

Cover of *Applied Imagination*.
From the author's collection.

It appears that the brainstorming method for which he is most famous was created in 1939, and it was first published in 1942 in his book *How to Think Up*. Based on this method, the U.S. Treasury came up with 103 ideas for selling Savings Bonds in a forty-minute session. Convinced of its merits, IBM and Dupont adopted the method and started training their employees in applying it.

So, what was Osborn's definition of brainstorming? "Using the brain to storm a creative problem— and doing so in commando fashion, with each stormer audaciously attacking the same objective." Groups did this by following three steps in the original writings, but a fourth was added in the various incarnations of *Applied Imagination*. On page 84 of the revised tenth edition, they are explained as follows:

(1) Criticism is ruled out. Adverse judgment of ideas must be withheld until later.

(2) "Free-wheeling" is welcomed. The wilder the idea, the better; it is easier to tame down than to think up.

(3) Quantity is wanted. The greater the number of ideas, the more the likelihood of winners.

(4) Combination and improvement are sought. In addition to contributing ideas of their own, participants should suggest how ideas of others can be turned into better ideas; or how two or more ideas can be joined into still another idea.

Osborn also recommended that facilitators be trained to manage sessions and that a scribe be appointed to take the notes. These two things are also standard practices in what are called "facilitated workshops" today; they are still used to solve a variety of business problems. One of the more popular stories about the early application of brainstorming was that, in just ninety minutes, a group of ten advertising men were able to create eighty-seven ideas on how to market a new drugstore.

Convinced he was on to something big, Osborn started the Creative Education Foundation (CEF) at the University of Buffalo in 1949. The foundation's charge was to "help educational agencies do more to develop creative potential." He thought that the education system of the day did a good job at making people critical but, in the balance, had stifled the creativity. As he stated, "Each of us has a creative mind that thinks up ideas and a judicial mind that criticizes them. The first trick is to keep these two minds from interfering with each other." The foundation ran a series of adult education programs in creativity, and soon afterward, similar programs were underway at Columbia, Drake, North Western, New York University and the University of Chicago.

Osborn continued to publish, and after he opened CEF, all his royalties went to the foundation. In 1955, the first Creative Problem Solving Institute (CPSI, pronounced "SIP-see") Conference was held in Buffalo. Sponsored by the foundation, this annual event continues to educate people on the creativity process. This year, 2020, the sixty-fifth annual CPSI Conference is scheduled to be held virtually and in-person in Buffalo.

Although he was not born in Buffalo, Osborn was always a strong promoter of the wonders of the area and was actively involved in the community. He was an avid golfer and participated in many golf events, often finishing near the top. He was even a member of the hallowed Augusta National Golf Club. He also served as director of both the Marine Trust Company (now HSBC) and Citizens Trust and as a trustee of the Western Savings Bank. He continued his loyalty to Hamilton College by serving as a trustee on its board. In the nonbusiness world, he belonged to the Westminster Presbyterian Church in Buffalo, was a member of both the University Club and the Buffalo Club and continued to summer at Bay Beach, where he had been married.

Tired of a constant drone in the press of what was bad about Buffalo, in 1948, Osborn penned a missive titled "What's Right About Buffalo." In it, he argued for all Buffalo citizens to focus on and be much more vocal about the things that made the city great. Many of these included the statements he gave back in 1911 in his speech about the six-cylindered city. Decades later, his grandson, John R. Osborn, wrote a follow up with updated facts.

After the publication of the booklet, Osborn used its content in a variety of speeches around town. One of those, in 1952, was reported in May 19 issue of the *Buffalo Evening News*:

> *Alex F. Osborn, the advertising man and author, answered the question "What's right about Buffalo?" in a talk before the Greater Buffalo Advertising Club. He urged Buffalonians to "count and recount" their community blessings*

and not "go out of their way to look for clouds and turn their backs on silver linings." The speech was in the tradition of the civic booster thumping for the hometown. This used to be a noble tradition until the intellectual snobs and other cynics spread the destructive notion that anyone who says nice things about the place he lives in is a boob and a Babbitt severely afflicted with "provincialism." Mr. Osborn, convinced that "a community appreciated by its own people is a better community in which to live," did a thorough job of summarizing the advantages of Buffalo-area living. He touched upon such factors as economic stability, home ownership, racial harmony, education, water supply, health and social welfare, climate, parks, zoo and recreation. We noted only one major omission. Mr. Osborn left out the further advantage of having at least a few people like himself to remind us now and then of the many benefits we as Buffalonians usually take for granted.

There would be no progress if communities were not self-critical and did not concentrate on the need for improvement. But there can be neither progress nor contentment if people are not conscious of achievements already attained, of foundations well-laid for further building.

A synopsis of his thoughts was republished in the July 4, 1960 issue of the *Buffalo Courier Express*:

Wouldn't our city be better off if we were more vocal about its virtues to those we meet on the road, to visitors within our gates, to our neighbors and to our youngsters? I make no plea for ballyhoo.

All I urge is that we count and re-count our blessings. By doing so, we will be happier—and we will even add to our advantages. For a community appreciated by its own people is a better community in which to live.

In addition to his numerous books and published speeches, in the 1960s, Osborn made a film called *Ideas by the Dozen*, and a series of records. A few years later, on May 5, 1966, Osborn died of cancer at the Roswell Park Memorial Institute in Buffalo, just short of his seventy-eighth birthday.

Osborn's brainstorming technique has been met with quite a bit of criticism over the years, which started nearly as soon as the technique was introduced. One of the earliest was a study conducted at 3M, which found that, given the same amount of time, individuals generated 30 to 40 percent more ideas—which were of better quality—than the groups. However, it is hard to say whether or not these prolific individuals would have been even more productive if they had been in a group. And, as Thomas Edison had

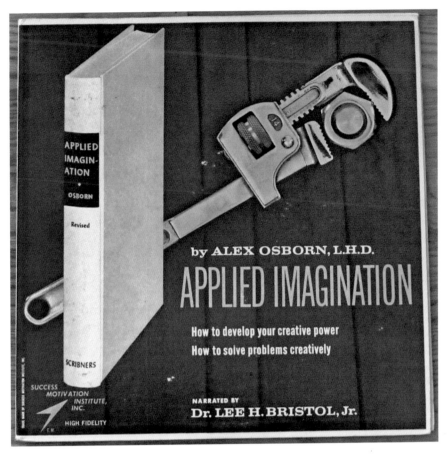

Cover of *Applied Imagination* records. *From the author's collection.*

learned with his Menlo Park team members, who numbered in the hundreds, teams worked better when a problem was divided into small tasks and each team member was solving a specific piece of a problem. Yet they still worked as a team when deciding what those tasks should be.

Despite all the denigration, nearly every worker today knows how to follow the brainstorming process, and they continue to do so. *Why?* Because it works. *Can other methods work more effectively?* Perhaps, but as long as the perceived problem is solved, does it matter? Osborn provided us with what was then a unique approach, and today, it is ubiquitous. The creativity-related organizations he founded continue to provide valuable training and ongoing research into the human creative process, and his firm BBDO is still a leading advertising agency. That's not a bad legacy.

10

ROBERT RICH AND NONDAIRY WHIPPED CREAM

Many inventions are accidents; such was the case with Robert Rich's frozen nondairy whipping cream. This chapter describes Rich's invention and the subsequent growth and leadership of Rich Products, which is, to this day, a major Buffalo employer.

Robert "Bob" Edward Rich, Sr. was born July 7, 1913, in Buffalo, New York, the son of Paul Jones Rich and Eleanor MacKenzie. He was the second-eldest son and had four siblings. His older brother was Paul Jr., and his other siblings were Willard, Arthur and Doris. His family owned a dairy and ice cream company. Rich attended Bennett High School and then studied at UB, graduating in 1935. That same year, his father loaned him $5,000, and with it, he purchased the Wilber (also spelled Wilbur) Farms Dairy. He spent the next few years building the farm from a "one horse, two truck" operation into the largest dairy company in western New York. Rich met Janet "Dolly" Ruth Webb at college, where he was captain of the UB football team for two years and founded the UB wrestling team. They attended the UB junior prom in 1934 and also eloped that year.

When World War II broke out, Rich's extensive experience in the dairy field was called on by the government. This announcement in the June 6, 1942 *Buffalo Evening News* explains:

> *Robert E. Rich, proprietor of the Wilber Farms Dairy, today was appointed to the War Production Board at Washington. He will be a business specialist in the dairy section. Mr. Rich, who was graduated in 1935 from the University of Buffalo, where he captained the varsity football and wrestling teams, will leave tomorrow night for Washington.*

The position pays $4,600 a year. Mr. Rich has been secretary of the Buffalo Dairy Council for three years.

In October the following year, Rich was transferred to Michigan, which changed his life and ultimately allowed him to virtually single-handedly create the nondairy frozen food industry. This simple promotion announcement in the *Courier Express* on October 24, 1943, did not in any way foreshadow this:

> *Robert E. Rich, 211 Lexington Avenue, former alternate administrator of the War Food Administration's ice cream section has been promoted to marketing agent for Detroit, Lansing, Flint and Saginaw, to handle the WFA's milk conservation program in the four cities. Rich, owner of Wilber Farms Dairy, 1149 Niagara Street, formerly was with the food distribution administration in its dairy branch and before that was with the War Production Board as a representative of independent milk dealers. He is expected at his new post, with offices in Detroit, Tuesday.*

Rich's work in Michigan did not go as smoothly as he had likely hoped it would. While serving in his post, Rich was involved in several controversies, involving the rationing, sale, production and availability of milk in the wartime Michigan cities. Rationing was blamed for leaving schools and hospitals without vital milk, and over-production was leading to the dumping, at times, of nearly one-third of the milk being produced. None of this, of course, was Rich's fault, but he was called out frequently in the Michigan press.

It was while working in Michigan that Rich had the opportunity to learn that Henry Ford and George Washington Carver were working on a nondairy milk made from soybeans at Ford's lab in his Greenfield Village complex in Dearborn, Michigan. There, Ford and his scientists had successfully created an alternative to rubber from goldenrod and had constructed a plastic car from soybeans.

Soybeans were not new to the United States at the time, but their use was still limited. They had been introduced to the United States in 1765 by Sam Bowen, who received some seeds from a Chinese source and planted them. He called them Chinese Vetch and used them to produce soy sauce. The first known use of the term *soybean* took place in 1804, when Dr. James Mease described the "liquid condiment" soy sauce as being produced from the soybean. In some Civil War documents, there are comments about roasting soybeans as a replacement for coffee, but the consumption of soybeans as a main food staple didn't gain traction until the 1930s.

Henry Ford had started experimenting with soybeans in the 1930s, and at the 1934 Chicago World's Fair, he served cheese and crackers, bread and butter, and milk and ice cream all made from soybeans. He and Carver were also using soybean byproducts as polymers. Rich became aware of all this when, as the story goes, a purchasing representative from Ford's hospital in Dearborn approached Rich about getting more butter for the hospital. Rich informed him that he was only in charge of milk, not butter. The Ford agent scoffed and replied that they had no need for milk and that all the milk and cream at the hospital was being produced from soybeans in the Carver lab. He invited Rich for a tour of the lab, which he eagerly agreed to.

While on the tour of the Carver Lab, Rich met several of the scientists who were conducting the soybean experiments, including Bob Smith, who, in 1944, produced the first commercial nondairy whipped cream called Delsoy. Rich also had an opportunity to see how the extraction process worked and was told he would be able to license it if he was interested in doing so.

On October 30, 1944, the *Detroit Free Press* announced:

> *Retiring after 2 1/2 years with the War Food Administration, Robert E. Rich, owner of the Wilber Farms Dairy, will resume management of the dairy. For the last year, he has been agent for the major milk markets in Michigan.*

While Rich had been in Washington and Michigan, his wife, Janet, had been running the dairy. When he returned, he immediately started working on a formula for soy cream. Dairy whipping cream was outlawed during the war, and Rich saw an opportunity to replace it with the soy cream. When his formula was perfected, he returned to Ford to negotiate his rights to the extraction process and was denied. Undeterred, he hired his own scientists and actually came up with a more efficient process, extracting 43 percent of the soy from the beans versus Ford's 30 percent. Although there are some discrepancies on exact dates, it appears that Rich Products was incorporated in November 1944, and the first product was on the market at the end of March 1945. The cream was called Whip Topping, and it was sold as a liquid in a cone-shaped half-pint container.

In the summer of 1945, the transformative "accident" took place. While packing up the cream on his way to demonstrate his product to a potential

Whip topping in the original cone shape. *Courtesy of the* Lansing State Journal, *September 15, 1946.*

customer, Rich used too much dry ice, and the cream froze. Since freezing ruins dairy cream, he was amazed when he whipped the frozen soy cream that it still whipped as it should, and he instantly realized the significance. He could freeze his cream and distribute it nationwide.

The first frozen versions of the cream were produced as early as October 1945 and definitely started shipping in January 1946. Rich, as Oishei, Carrier and Osborn did before him, understood that marketing his product was key. That same month, it was advertised in *Quick Frozen Foods*: "A New Frozen Food! Whip Topping is a frozen pure-soy cream for whipping and baking." Later in 1946, other advertisements ran in *Soybean Digest* with headings such as "Whip Topping by Plane to Alaska." The December 1946 issue provided a nice profile of the company and talked about the contents of the cream: "Whip Topping is a pure frozen soy cream containing soy protein, vegetable fats, carbohydrates, salt, flavoring, and coloring."

Rich's press coverage for his product was good, but it was not the only coverage he was getting. Although it was probably not humorous to him at the time, the October 8, 1946 issue of the *Buffalo Courier Express* carried an interesting nonproduct-related story about Rich:

The telephone number of Mrs. Josephine Tracy Rose, 38-year-old divorcee who was found slain Saturday in the basement laundry room of an apartment house here, was listed in the name of Robert E. Rich of Buffalo, police disclosed tonight. Police said Rich, here on a business trip, told them he knew the dead woman and once planned to rent the apartment she occupied. He said the telephone number was listed in his name because of his intended occupancy but that when he did not take the apartment, the telephone was left for Mrs. Rose without a change being made in the holder's name. Police said there is "not the slightest hint" the Buffalo man was involved in the killing.

Just a month later, on November 20, 1946, Rich received potentially devastating news; the government had lifted its ban on the sale of milk-based whipping cream. The company had just built expanded production facilities, and nearly overnight, sales plummeted. Rich turned again to marketing to regain sales.

In early 1947, the company started running advertisements in *Good Housekeeping, Parents Magazine, Life* and other popular lifestyle and news magazines. The approach paid off. The 1947 volume of *Food Packer* included this announcement:

> *"Topper," the little gentleman who serves as trademark for the new frozen soybean cream, Whip Topping, made by Rich Products Corporation of Buffalo, N.Y., has been decorated again. This time it's the seal of approval from the Union of Orthodox Rabbis, awarded to Whip Topping and establishing Whip Topping as a "Kosher Parve" among frozen food products. This latest stamp of approval follows closely on the awards won by Whip Topping from Good Housekeeping and Parents Magazine.*

Rich Product's Whip Topping was purportedly the first nondairy product to receive these designations, and by this time, the company was producing one million pints monthly and couldn't keep up, so it enlarged its facilities again.

Sales continued to grow. The company's sales in the first ten months of 1948 surpassed all of 1947's sales by about 40 percent. The product was also getting great press. A long profile in the February 1949 issue of *Quick Frozen Foods* talked about the history of the company, its marketing approach and its production facilities.

> *The topping is packed in a container which has become identified with the product through its trademark and shape. The decision to use the Pur Pak container was made because the square shape takes little space and can be nested. It is a sturdy package and cannot be damaged in the display cabinet. It is coated inside and out with paraffine [sic] for protection and to prevent leakage. At the Rich plant, the package is received in the form of printed blanks and the package is folded, glued and waxed, filled and sealed all in one operation on one machine.*

It is interesting that this profile comments on the use of Pur Pak containers (also referred to as Pure-Pak) because when Rich first approached the company about its packaging, it refused to sell to a "nondairy" product company. This changed in late 1946, when the new packaging was announced in a number of newspaper advertisements. The trademarked Topper, referred to above, was actually a caricature of the new containers. Once packaged, the filled cartons were placed in wire baskets and then taken to the blast room for freezing. When frozen, they were ready for distribution and sales. The same profile in 1949 notes how Rich Products supported its Whip Topping:

> *Demonstrations built around the "Topper" trademark, which has become an integral part of the company's advertising, are conducted at all hotel, dietetic and other trade expositions and shows. Dealers are supplied with window streamers, decals, point of sale tape, folders and other selling aids.*

Unfortunately, this popularity caused problems for the company, as it began to be sued by numerous dairy-heavy states for selling an illegal imitation dairy product. State senators, especially in dairy states like Iowa, were also lobbying against nondairy products. A profile of Rich in the December 18, 1949 edition of the *Buffalo Courier Express* had a humorous response to the senators: "Mr. Rich often wonders what would be the reaction of senators from our great dairy states if they knew that Whip Topping has been used, for the last four years, in the cafeteria in the U.S. Senate."

Rich challenged all of these comments and fought the legal cases, and he purportedly won forty of the forty-one brought against him. His formal rebuttal was very clever, as it tried to tie Henry Ford back to the mix. He justified his product by saying it was not an imitation but a replacement, just as the Model T did not imitate horses but replaced them.

As he continued to win cases, Rich was also gaining competition from other nondairy product producers, and the simple name of Whip Topping was becoming ubiquitous. To continue to differentiate his groundbreaking product from the rest of the market, in 1950, the name Rich's Whip Topping replaced the original Whip Topping nomenclature.

Whip Topping with "Topper" in Pur-Pak. *Courtesy of the* Atlanta Constitution, *October 3, 1947.*

Throughout the 1950s, Rich Products expanded its product line. It formed a subsidiary company called Richzert and introduced a soy dessert called Chil-Zert circa 1951, but the product did not sell well. The ice cream distributors that had the proper freezing units to transport the product refused to do so, and the other frozen food distributors couldn't keep it frozen well enough. It would thaw, refreeze and become crystalized, just like thawed and refrozen ice cream does, and that ruined the taste and texture. After the FDA seized a shipment in New Orleans, the company quietly stopped making it. In 1955, the company started selling frozen eclairs that were filled with its whipped topping, and in May 1956, it introduced a non-soybean coconut oil–based version of Whip Topping, and later, it introduced a version in an "automatic" dispenser can.

The expansion of products required more space, and in the August 28, 1959 *Buffalo Courier Express*, the following announcement was made:

> *The Canada Dry Bottling Co. of Buffalo plant, 1148 Niagara St., has been sold to Robert E. Rich, president of Rich Products Co. and of Wilbur Farms Dairy, whose facilities are located across the street. President George J. Meyer of Canada Dry Bottling said his firm has until August 1960 to vacate but expects to be out of its present location long before that. "We are currently studying three other sites on which we have options, and expect to make a decision within ten days," he said. The Canada Dry building is owned by the 1148 Niagara St. Corp., whose president is Norman Ernst. Adjacent to the building is a 15,000 square foot parking lot.*

Rich's really needed the new facilities after it released what is now considered its second flagship product, Coffee Rich, that same year. Coffee Rich was billed as a "coffee whitener," not a cream, in an attempt to avoid the same legal problems it had fought with Whip Topping, but alas, the attempt was unsuccessful. Throughout the early 1960s, the company faced more legal challenges, which it continued to win, using the same argument that Coffee Rich replaced cream, it did not imitate it. Coffee Rich was advertised in a variety of ways, including as artwork on West Bend coffee pots.

In 1964, the company built a plant in Fort Erie, Canada, for the Rich Products of Canada subsidiary, and its vice-president was Robert E. Rich Jr., who had been born to the Riches in 1941. By 1966, the company was considered an industry giant. Another profile in *Quick Frozen Foods* marked the company's twenty-first anniversary with photographs of Rich Sr. and Rich Jr.,

Above: Rich's Whip Topping in an automatic dispenser. *From the author's collection.*

Left: Rich's Coffee Rich advertising on a West Bend coffee pot. *From the author's collection.*

the U.S. and Canadian plants and several of the products. That profile was summarized in the February 13, 1966 issue of the *Buffalo Courier Express*:

> *The Rich Products Corp., another Buffalo headquartered firm was the subject of a recent feature article in Quick Frozen Foods Magazine, the "bible" of that industry. Now in its 21st year of operation, the company rose from a tiny firm producing a "wartime replacement" whip topping in 1945, to a giant of the industry today with a broadly diversified line of frozen products. Total sales in 1945 were 128,000, while sales in the frozen food industry were less than $200 million. Now, Rich's sales top $25 million annually, while the frozen food industry has expanded to more than $5 billion in yearly sales.*

Robert (Bob) Rich Jr. and Robert (Bob) Rich Sr. *From Rich Product's collection.*

The firm continued to grow throughout the next decade, and when Robert Rich Sr. retired in 1978, Robert Rich Jr. took over the corporate reins. By then, the company had plants in California, Pennsylvania, Ohio and New Jersey, in addition to the Buffalo and Fort Erie plants, and was producing a variety of packaged frozen foods in addition to its two staples.

The 1980s saw more growth, largely from buyouts of other frozen food companies, a pattern that remains today. In 1990, Rich was one of the first four people inducted into the National Frozen Food Industry's Hall of Fame. Rich's wife, the former Janet Webb, died in 1998, and Rich died on February 13, 2006, in Palm Beach, Florida.

With what ended up being a very lucky break from his soy cream freezing on the way to his 1945 product demonstration, Rich became a pioneer in two industries: frozen foods and nondairy products. The company he started seventy-five years ago continues to innovate in both those industries, provides jobs to about 1,500 local associates and more than 10,000 associates worldwide. It is also a major donor to a variety of local charities. Rich took the company from a one-product company based on the "miracle cream from the soybean" to an international giant. It was a miracle, indeed.

11

WILSON GREATBATCH AND THE PACEMAKER

B y the mid-1900s, Buffalo had lost much of its dominance in the nation. Although the city's population had grown to more than 500,000 people, its rank in the United States continued to decline. Yet Buffalo's inventiveness did not wane, as the area continued to inspire the creativity of residents. This chapter explains Wilson Greatbatch's creation of the implantable pacemaker and the business that grew from his work.

On September 6, 1919, Wilson "Bill" Greatbatch was born to Walter Plant Greatbatch and Charlotte "Lottie" Margaret Recktenwalt in Buffalo, New York. Greatbatch's father, Walter, was a foreman in the steel mills that were booming at that time. His mother worked as a secretary. When Greatbatch was born, the nation was still recovering from World War I, Woodrow Wilson had been reelected as the U.S. president, an influenza pandemic was devastating the nation, there were several union strikes and Prohibition had just been ratified. Greatbatch's parents chose Wilson as his first name in honor of one of their heroes, Woodrow Wilson. Greatbatch went to West Seneca High School and graduated in 1936. He had always been interested in technology; throughout his early years, he was a member of Buffalo's "Jolly Juniors" Club and was active in scouting. He got his HAM radio license at the age of sixteen.

Some of his early notoriety came in 1938, when he combined those two interests. Greatbatch was instrumental in setting up radio communications between the Boy Scouts "Southhaven" camp in Freedom, New York, about fifty miles south of Buffalo, and the Buffalo scouting headquarters. The July 16, 1938 issue of the *Buffalo Evening News* reported on this event.

> *On last Wednesday morning, a communication by radio from Bill Greatbatch, the radio engineer at Scouthaven to Sherwood Beutler, radio adviser to the Sea Scout Radio Division, made it possible for Buffalo Scout Headquarters to get orders for supplies such as merit badges and awards and foodstuffs for the commissary in rapid time. No longer do the orders have to be carried in by car or mail but are rushed immediately to the radio and then sent by code directly to Buffalo, which is a matter of minutes. This is an innovation in the camping procedure for 1938—a dream long planned for, at last come true. This radio communication from Scouthaven to Buffalo is not peculiar to Scouthaven, for the boys and men on the Sea Scout Ship Polaris maintain constant communication with the Sea Scout Base.*

Greatbatch continued to participate in scouting, moving from patrol leader for Scout Troop 53 in his younger years, to a Scouthaven staff member in 1938 and to assistant scout director by 1939. In 1940, he was helping scouts learn Morse code with a weekly radio broadcast.

When the United States became involved in World War II, Greatbatch enlisted in the navy and held a variety of electronics and radio-related positions. In October 1941, he was serving in the Third Naval District on the SS *Oneida*. He also served as the radio operator on the USS *Melville*. He briefly taught radar techniques to fellow servicemen and even did a stint on the USS *Monterey* aircraft carrier, flying in combat missions as a rear gunner. While Greatbatch was on the *Monterey*, future president Gerald Ford was serving as a deck officer, and another future president, George Bush, was a torpedo plane pilot on the *Monterey*'s sister ship, the USS *San Jacinto*. Ever the student, according to a profile on Greatbatch in the June 11, 1970 *Wellsville Daily Reporter*, while in the military, he took courses at "Buffalo State Teacher's College, Providence College, the University of Wisconsin and the University of Texas."

On January 1, 1945, Greatbatch married his high school sweetheart, Eleanor Fay Wright, in King, Washington, and when, later that year, he was honorably discharged, the couple moved back to Buffalo. He worked for a year at the New York Telephone Company and then decided to make use of his GI Bill benefits and attend Cornell University. As Greatbatch noted in interviews and speeches after his success, he had had trouble getting admitted to Cornell because there were no dormitories available for "non-

Wilson Greatbatch's marriage license. *From Washington Marriage Records, 1854–2013, Washington State Archives.*

resident" students, so he purchased a farm in Danby, New York, just south of Cornell, and was then admitted as a resident student.

Greatbatch graduated from Cornell in 1950 and took graduate courses there for a year while also providing electronics work on the animals in Cornell's Animal Behavior Farm. This was where he purportedly became interested in the function of human hearts, because of what he learned from the medical students and staff he met there.

In 1953, Greatbatch founded the Buffalo–Niagara Chapter subgroup of the Institute of Radio Engineers (IRE) called the Professional Group on Medical Electronics. He chaired the chapter for two years and was associated with it for decades.

Wilson Greatbatch's discharge. *From the U.S. WWII draft cards of young men, 1940–1947, National Archives.*

He continued his education at the University of Buffalo (UB), earning a master's degree in 1956. Although several later profiles stated that his degree came in 1957, he is listed in the June 7, 1956 issue of the *Buffalo Evening News* as having received his degree that month. Greatbatch also taught at UB and worked at Cornell Aeronautical Laboratory (CAL), the Curtiss research spinoff mentioned earlier. There, he discovered transistors for the first time; those miniaturized electronic devices that ultimately replaced large, bulky vacuum tubes.

While teaching at UB, Greatbatch was already conducting heart-related research. As a May 30, 1957 article in the *Buffalo Courier Express* noted, "Professor Wilson Greatbatch…is working with Dr. Simon Rodbard of the UB Chronic Disease Institute to devise and develop better and more precise electronic instrumentation to determine and analyze heart sounds." The next day, Greatbatch made the *Buffalo Evening News* again with this announcement: "The University of Buffalo has been granted a construction permit by the Federal Communications Commission for a new non-commercial, educational FM radio station. Prof. Wilson Greatbatch would be in charge of the station, which would operate on 88.7 megacycles with power of 185 watts." WBFO, as the station is now known, still operates as the public radio station for Buffalo, although it has moved off the UB campus.

Greatbatch left CAL after graduating from UB and took a job at Taber Instrument Corporation, an electronics company based near Buffalo in North Tonawanda. An article in the *Buffalo Evening News* on August 29, 1957, explained the importance of Taber's work on medical and military components. "Transistors, tiny pieces of germanium or silicon about the size of the head of a carpet tack, perform the amplifying job formerly done by the tubes, and they do the work better. Taber, a producer of electronic components for missiles, is experienced in the use of transistors." The company manufactured the heart-monitoring equipment for the space program, and Greatbatch was in charge of the transistor department there.

It was while working at Taber Instrument that Greatbatch had his inspirational "accident." He had been working on building an oscillator to measure heartbeats, and when he used the wrong resistor, the machine started to generate its own electric pulses. Because of his ongoing interest in the human heart and his understanding of how it functioned, he immediately recognized that he could use something like this to simulate a heartbeat. He turned his research to creating an implantable electronic pacemaker.

Despite Greatbatch's enthusiasm about the possibilities, he found it difficult to convince others. The doctors he contacted at Buffalo's Chronic Disease Research Institute showed no interest in such a device. Some of the problem was that many people thought pacemakers would hurt more than help. The risks of the surgery that was needed to implant them, along with the risk of infection afterward, were high. And Greatbatch wasn't the first to propose pacemakers. As early as 1850, French neurologist Guillaume Duchene had been experimenting with electrical muscle stimulation. Although Duchene was best known for using his "stimulating coil" to get people to change their facial expressions, in 1869, he successfully used it to slow the heartbeat of a woman whose heart was racing dangerously fast. In 1952, Dr. Paul Zoll built the first external pacemaker, but the unit was very large, and it was not transportable. While it saved people's lives, it also made them immobile. However, the delay in finding a surgeon who was willing to attempt the pacemaker implants meant that Greatbatch missed the window for being the first to use an implantable pacemaker. On October 8, 1958, Dr. Ake Senning and Rune Elmqvist from Sweden had that honor. Over the years, Greatbatch and Elmqvist became close colleagues.

Finally, in 1959, Greatbatch convinced Dr. William Chardack and his lab assistant, Andrew Gage, with whom Greatbatch had attended high school, that his idea had merit. Then, the trio moved quickly, and just three weeks later, they tried the device in a dog—it worked, albeit briefly. The first dog lived only minutes after the successful operation, but subsequent experiments were able to prolong the longevity of the device in the animals. (It is important to note that some sources state this successful operation on a dog occurred on May 7, 1958, which would have predated the Swiss tests on a human.)

In November 1959, the trio, often referred to as the "Bow-Tie Team" because they all preferred wearing bow ties, announced their success with the animals. The story was carried via the *New York Times*'s wire service nationwide to more than three dozen papers, including those located in Louisville, Miami, Minneapolis and even Missouli, Montana. Greatbatch, Chardack and Gage continued to conduct experiments on dogs, and within a year, they had refined the device enough that the dogs were able to live for months rather than hours. They decided the pacemaker was ready to try on a human subject, and the first to be placed in a human was implanted in April 1960. An extensive article, with accompanying photos of the device and happy patients, in the *Buffalo Evening News* on September 23, 1960, described the first and subsequent operations:

> *A 77-year-old man worked happily in his East Side garden today with no fear of the blackouts that plagued him for more than a year. On the other side of the city, a 36-year-old husband and father, unable to work for 18 months, went cheerfully off to school to learn to be a beautician. Both men had suffered from a condition known as complete heart block. Their heartbeats were too slow to sustain normal activities. They have been given a new lease on life by a small electronic "pacemaker" buried under the skin at their waistlines. The device, including its batteries, is about the size of a pocket watch. It stimulates their hearts to beat fast enough to avoid disabling attacks of unconsciousness and permit moderate physical activity.*
>
> *The older man, Frank Henafelt of 371 May St., is the first patient in medical history in whom a physiological disorder has been successfully corrected on a long-term basis by a completely implanted electronic device independent of outside sources of power....Before the pacemaker was implanted, Mr. Henafelt's heart was beating only 32 times a minute, as compared to a normal of about 80 during waking hours. His first blackout came in a neighborhood bank. Four others followed within a year. After one fractured his skull, he took to wearing a football helmet to prevent further head injuries. On April 18, at Millard Fillmore Hospital, a team of surgeons from that hospital and the Veterans Hospital opened his chest and placed a bipolar electrode patch on the outside of the right ventricle or pumping chamber of his heart.*

Wilson Greatbatch holding a pacemaker. *From the University Archives, University at Buffalo, the State University of New York.*

Two stainless-steel wires emerging from the surface of this small flat silicone rubber patch penetrated the surface of the heart muscle. The wires from the electrode were brought out through the chest wall and connected to an external pacemaker whose rate and amplitude could be controlled. The rate was set at 48 beats a minute. For more than two months, the surgical team watched Mr. Henafelt as he adjusted to his new heart rate. His blackouts ceased. On June 8, the team decided that it was safe to implant a pacemaker. They disconnected the external device and soldered the electrode wires to the terminals of an internal model. The junction was covered with quick-setting silicone rubber that firmly bound the capsule of the pacemaker, also enclosed in silicone rubber, to the silicone sleeve surrounding the two wires. The pacemaker was then sterilized and implanted. The actual implantation is so simple that it is done under local anesthesia.

In June 1961, Greatbatch was still at working at Taber as the manager of the aerospace medicine division, and he spoke at the University of Rochester on monitoring the recording of physiological measurements. Soon afterward, he left his job at Taber, and with only $2,000 in startup funding, began developing the units in his barn. He said that he built fifty over a two-year span; forty of these were used in animals and ten were used in human subjects. By the end of 1961, he had had nineteen patients, and sixteen lived for more than a few weeks. The article on that milestone was printed in more than one hundred newspapers, and in 1962, Greatbatch received his patent on the device.

While waiting for the patent, Greatbatch formed Wilson Greatbatch Inc. and licensed production of the devices to Medtronic Inc., a medical device manufacturer based in Minnesota. He served on their board from 1961 to 1968 and ultimately sold his patents to them in 1967. In 1963, Wilson Greatbatch Inc. merged to become Mennen-Greatbatch. Greatbatch started a new company, Wilson Greatbatch Ltd., in 1970, and it focused on producing pacemaker batteries. It was ultimately located at 10000 Wherle Drive in Clarence. When he announced his discovery of an updated lithium battery in September 1975, the article was carried in more than two dozen papers. By that time, two hundred thousand people, including actors Henry Fonda and Peter Sellers and Supreme Court judge William O. Douglas had pacemakers. The company agreed to sell to a new medical company that was forming in Minnesota in 1977, but the deal fell through. By 1981, the number of pacemaker recipients had grown to more than three hundred thousand.

Throughout the 1970s, 1980s and 1990s, Greatbatch spoke all over the country on panels and as a keynote speaker. He also donated to and taught at Houghton College for a number of years, starting in 1970. He turned the company over to his son, Warren, in 1985. In one of his talks, in 1990, he noted that the thirty-six-year-old recipient noted above was still alive and doing well, thirty years after his operation.

While these early pacemakers were considered miraculous, they were not without their faults. The major problem faced with early pacemakers was the stability of the electrodes. A variety of metals were tried, but ultimately, it was a platinum-iridium spring coil electrode developed by Dr. Chardack that was determined to be most effective. This became the basis of the Medtronic Model 5814 pacemaker.

Another issue was with the life of the battery. The earlier batteries lasted about two years, but duration continued to improve as new types of batteries were developed. The longest battery life came from lithium batteries, and although many pacemaker manufacturers were slow to move to the new batteries because they required a change in the pacemaker design itself, by 1990, lithium batteries were the industry standard.

An interesting side experiment for Greatbatch was in the creation of nuclear batteries. Greatbatch and Chardack designed several pacemakers that used plutonium as its power source. They started using these in 1970, and by 1975, there were five hundred pacemakers running on plutonium, but getting approval to use the plutonium and the excessive cost ($5,000 versus $1,000) proved to not be worth the effort, and they were never mass-produced.

Because the devices needed to be implanted, it was critical that they be sterilized so as not to introduce infections. There were five main ways to sterilize the devices, which included steaming, cold chemical sterilization, radiation, ethylene oxide gas and heat in excess of 150 degrees Celsius. Greatbatch preferred the use of steam.

By the 1990s, Wilson Greatbatch Ltd. had grown to have 800 employees with plants around the world. In 1997, the company was sold, and by 1998, Wilson Greatbatch Ltd. employed 650 people and was the world's largest supplier of pacemaker batteries. The company's name was changed to Greatbatch Inc. in 2005.

In his later years, Greatbatch turned his interests to solving the AIDS epidemic and the worldwide energy problem. He advocated for better blood screening to filter AIDS from transfusion banks and planted acres of poplar trees, which mature in about seven years, trying to come up with a renewable fuel source. He also supported solar energy and designed and built a solar-powered canoe, which he piloted on a more-than-one-hundred-mile trip in the Erie Barge Canal and Finger Lakes. He also promoted building stations on the moon to harvest helium-3 as an oil substitute.

By 2000, it was estimated that there were three million people living active lives with pacemakers, and more than 500,000 were implanted every year. Greatbatch and his wife had been married for more than sixty-five years

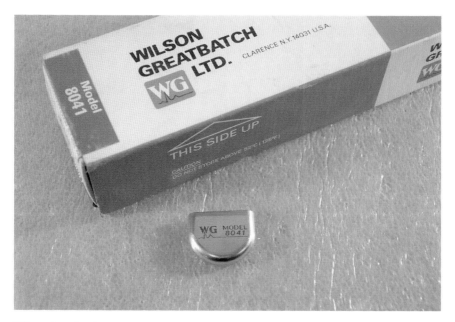

Wilson Greatbatch Ltd. battery. *From the author's collection.*

when he died on September 27, 2011, at the age of ninety-two; they had five children. Greatbatch had earned many prestigious awards, garnered more than two hundred patents and had donated enough money to Houghton College for them to erect five new buildings.

Although, like Holly, not all of all of Greatbatch's inventions and ideas for the future panned out, those that did were highly successful. His pacemakers saved lives, and the batteries he perfected went on to revolutionize the battery industry as well. As Greatbatch himself noted in a 1998 interview printed in the March 1 issue of the *South Idaho Press* newspaper and many others, "Nine things out of 10 won't work. The 10th one will pay for the other nine." He was a deeply religious man with high hopes for the future, and he inspired the next generations of inventors. As he first noted in a commencement address to Clarkson University in 1987 and repeated many times in articles after that, "Don't fear failure. Don't crave success. The reward is not in the results, but rather in the doing."

12

FRANK AND TERESSA BELLISSIMO AND CHICKEN WINGS

Perhaps Buffalo's most famous "invention," Buffalo wings, were created by Frank and Teressa Bellissimo in their restaurant, the Anchor Bar. This chapter portrays the various creation stories and discusses the role this "invention" has had on appetizers throughout the world.

Buffalo reached its peak population in the 1950s, boasting 580,132 people, making it the fourteenth-largest city in the United States. As noted in earlier chapters, its location on Lake Erie had made it a perfect spot for the early grain industry, and shipping—and later, railroads—continued to keep the city in the nation's forefront. But by the 1960s, Buffalo had started to decline in population, and the downtown core was deteriorating as the suburbs continued to grow. The opening of the St. Lawrence Seaway in 1959 had allowed the shipping fleets to bypass Buffalo. Manufacturing had started to move south and to foreign countries, and, as it was throughout the country, Buffalo had its share of civil unrest with the desegregation of schools and protests against the Vietnam War. Yet the steel industry and the automobile-related industries remained strong, at least until the mid-1970s, and there was a growing recognition of Buffalo's arts and theater community. This was the Buffalo that gave birth to the now–world famous "Buffalo wings."

Francesco (Frank) Bellissimo was the youngest of six children, and was born on June 16, 1896, in Palermo, Sicily, in Italy to Dominic and Angeline Bellissimo. According to the 1900 census, Frank and his family had moved to the United States and were residing in Buffalo. Teressa (also spelled Theresa, Theressa and Teresa) was born November 18, 1900, also in Palermo, Sicily, in Italy. Her father was John (Giovanni) Guzzo (Guzzio) and her mother was Mary (Maria) Gambino. She was the sixth of seven children and came with her parents to the United States in 1904. By 1920, her father had died, and Teressa was living in Buffalo with her mother and two sisters. Her elder sister was working as a seamstress, and Teressa and her younger sister were working as box builders in a powder shop. At that time, Frank was working as a coal salesman and living with his brother Stephen. He also had jobs at his father's butcher shop and at a gas company. Frank and Teressa started dating when he was sixteen, and they finally married on June 27 in either 1919 or 1920. The 1920 New York State marriage index says a Frank Bellissinio, easily a misspelling of Bellissimo, was married on June 27, although the couple celebrated their fiftieth anniversary in 1969.

The couple had their only child, a son named Dominic (sometimes called Donald, Don and Dom), on November 22, 1924. According to the 1930 census, Frank Bellissimo managed a restaurant in 1930, and during the 1930s, he, along with Teressa, worked at a restaurant known as the Anchor Grill that they owned with Frank's brother Stephen, first at 122 Main Street and then at 27–29 Main Street. (Although, in an interview in 1969, they gave the address as 19 Main Street, business paperwork shows the 27–29 address.) In July 1939, Stephen passed away, and in 1940, Frank and Teressa opened their own tavern and restaurant called the Anchor Bar and Grill at 1047 Main Street in Buffalo. An announcement in the December 24, 1940 edition of the *Buffalo Evening News*, under the heading of "Night Clubs," noted:

> *Frank and Theresa, formerly of the Anchor Grill, have opened their own new spot, the Anchor Bar, at Main and North Streets, the entire place being decorated in nautical style, with many accessories of boats on display. The music is furnished by Halley and her band with entertainment along novelty lines being featured.*

Prior to that fateful night of the creation of Buffalo wings, the restaurant served Italian cuisine and was a popular nightspot for many of the city's Italian residents. The Bellissimos lived in an apartment above the bar. As the name implies, the restaurant was decorated in a nautical theme, with lanterns, anchors, ropes and other nautical paraphernalia, including a real rowboat that patrons could row. It provided entertainment on the weekends and sometimes during the week. Teressa and her sister, Florence, often performed there, as did Frank and myriad local, regional and national names. One of the patrons' favorite songs, as noted in the June 10, 1938 column "Around the Clubs" in the *Buffalo Evening News*, was Teressa's rendition of a song she called "The Butcher Boy," her take on an Italian

Frank and Teressa Bellissimo's wedding photo. *From Karen Caputo Kiekbusch's collection.*

ballad with her own words. It became so popular, in fact, that that same year, the internationally known singer Rudy Vallee, who was a frequent Anchor Bar patron, copied down the words and added it to his act.

Several entertainers who went to New York City in the 1940s to perform in Carnegie Hall and other venues were hailed in news reports as "alumni" of the Anchor Bar. The couple was also active in local politics, sponsored a bowling team in local and out of town league competitions for many years and, during World War II, advertised no charge for servicemen.

Their advertisements were in nearly every weekly issue of both the *Buffalo Evening News* and the *Buffalo Courier Express* and were nestled on the "amusements" pages among advertisements for *Gone with the Wind*, Shirley Temple and Betty Davis movies and Kay Jeweler advertisements for diamond solitaire rings that were sold at $19.75. They held New Years, Halloween and Christmas parties for patrons, charging $1.50 per person. Although the bar was one of only about ten nightclub advertisers in 1936, there were more than two dozen clubs advertising in 1945. Some of the Anchor Bar newspaper advertisements had anchors, others had steering wheels or rope. Many of the advertisements had their taglines "Ring the bell and row the boat" and "Food fit for a king." Whether intentional or not, when listed alphabetically in advertisements in the newspapers, their name of Anchor Bar got them always listed first. Not surprisingly, the music during the 1930s and 1940s was advertised as jazz and swing.

During the 1950s and 1960s, the bar continued to be a popular nightspot. In November 1954, the Polish Arts Club was having Liberace play, and Frank and Teressa were featuring local musicians, such as the Pastels. As popular music changed, so did the acts at the Anchor Bar. It often hosted Latin American musicians, comedy acts and dancers. It introduced Ladies Nights to encourage more business, and in 1961, it had an act "Featuring the Latest Dance Craze From New York's Peppermint Club: THE TWIST."

An extensive profile in the *Buffalo Courier Express* on July 6, 1969, describes the Bellissimos' relationship, other festivities and stars at the Anchor Bar over the years. It was also this article that supported the Rude Vallee story from 1938. The following is a piece of that article:

Theirs is a loud, laughable, loving, quarrelsome, but always entertaining companionship that operates 18 hours a day with all their patrons invited to participate in their ebullient comradery. When Theresa isn't yelling at Frank, she is belting out songs and vice versa. Theresa sings better than Frank, oftener and louder and attracts famous musicians and entertainers like bees to a hive. Famous bandsmen and headliners have haunted her establishment for food, fun and, as she says, "to steal my songs." Ted Lewis made Frank and Theresa's restaurant a port of call whenever he came to Buffalo. Frank Sinatra used to sing songs for their patrons when he was just a little-known crooner with Harry James' band. The Dorseys, Sammy Davis Jr., Edna Day, Joe Guercio, Hank Jones, Oscar Peterson, Maynard Ferguson, the McGuire Sisters, Jimmy Smith—all the rag-time and rock 'n roll greats pass the word along that the place to go, when in Buffalo, is the Bellissimo's Anchor Bar.

Left: A large display advertisement for the Anchor Bar. *Courtesy of the* Buffalo Evening News, *December 5, 1944.*

Right: Teressa Bellissimo. *From Karen Caputo Kiekbusch's collection.*

Prior to the creation of "Buffalo wings"—and even today—eating the wings from a roasted or barbecued whole chicken had always been popular, but when chicken was fried or otherwise prepared in different cut pieces, the wings were often disposed of or used for stock along with the backs and necks—that is, until 1964, when Teressa created her version of wings. Chicken wings have three components; drumettes, flats and tips, but generally, only the two larger drumettes and flats are used for Buffalo wings.

How the Anchor Bar's version of wings was created is a matter up for discussion, but the general gist is that Dominic Bellissimo, the owners' son, was bartending around closing on a Friday night in 1964, when some of his friends arrived and were hungry. Teressa didn't have any "real" food left, so she took the chicken wings that were to have become stock later and put them in the deep fryer. After they were cooked, she added butter and other ingredients to some Franks Red Hot Sauce, tossed the wings in the sauce and served them with a blue cheese dip and celery on the side. Variants on the story include that the original wings were broiled, not fried; that there were extra wings because a vendor had delivered wings for stock rather than backs and necks; and that Dominic wanted to treat the customers to a meat dish because it was after midnight and the Catholics could eat meat again.

Some critics of these various origin stories say that, in fact, two different restaurants served wings this way before the Anchor Bar. The most commonly cited story is that John Young, at his Buffalo restaurant called Wings 'n Things, created a special sauce he called a "Mambo" (or "Mombo") sauce that he served on his breaded, fried, whole chicken wings. His sauce was also a hot sauce, and his claim dates to 1964.

Very little of the bar's advertising after 1964 mentioned the wings. Only one Anchor Bar advertisement from 1966 has been located that mentioned wings, and in that advertisement, the wings were referred to as barbecued chicken wings in a list of four specialties. Whatever version of the creation story is true doesn't really matter because, whatever their origin, the wings at the Anchor Bar were a hit, and people started coming to the restaurant just for the wings. This was great for business because, at that time, wings were very inexpensive, and the hot sauce made for thirsty customers.

By 1973, other Buffalo restaurants had started advertising their own versions of what were then being called "Buffalo wings," and the Anchor Bar was selling three thousand pounds of wings every week. In 1977, when then-mayor Stanley Makowski declared July 29 as "Chicken Wings Day," the Anchor Bar was selling four thousand pounds per week, and it was estimated that the city was selling $15,000 to $20,000 per day in wing orders, which were sold at $2.10 per serving of ten. Former residents, including several Buffalo Bills players, had wings flown in for parties, and Janice Okun, the *Buffalo News* food columnist, predicted that the dish would eventually spread nationwide. She was certainly right.

Although they were originally referred to as barbecued wings, the most popular versions of wings are made with a type of hot sauce in three styles: mild, medium and hot. The Anchor Bar made its own blue cheese dressing as well and experimented with baking and barbecuing the wings before settling on frying them in peanut oil.

Many people in the 1970s encouraged the Bellissimos to crack down on copycats by starting franchises, licensing the recipe or doing other types of promotions, but, as Frank noted, he was in his eighties by then; business at the restaurant was doing well, and he was happy with that.

Frank Bellissimo died on October 22, 1980; he was eighty-four. That same year, while on the campaign trail, Senator Walter Mondale purportedly ordered five hundred wings to be delivered to his plane while he was in town. In 1981, an arsonist set a fire in a rear storage area of the restaurant;

that fire spread to the upstairs apartment where Teressa and her nurse were sleeping. They were both rescued by a restaurant employee. The fire caused about $70,000 worth of damage to the building and its contents; however, the bar only remained closed for a few days before reopening.

Chicken wings were honored again in 1984, when, during a week of celebrating in Buffalo, two senators and the Buffalo mayor, Jimmy Griffin, declared the day Chicken Wings Day in Washington, D.C. By then, wings were not just being sold in taverns but in high-end restaurants and in bars in Washington, D.C.; New York City; and many other places.

Teressa Bellissimo died on November 11, 1985. She was also eighty-four at the time of her death but had been confined to her bed in the apartment since she had suffered a stroke ten years earlier. By the time of their deaths, Dominic was running the restaurant, and he continued to do so until his sudden death in 1991. In 1986, he launched a massive press campaign via the Associated Press (AP), which featured a photo of Dom holding a plate of wings that was reprinted in more than four dozen newspapers. The caption accompanying that photograph called Bellissimo "Rooster," an appropriate nickname. By 1987, the Anchor Bar was selling eight thousand pounds of wings per week at $3.78 per ten pieces—which was really only five wings. The city's total wings sales had increased to thirty-five thousand pounds per week, with the Anchor Bar still the first in sales volume, as it was responsible for about 25 percent of that market. In 1989, Dominic Bellissimo announced the launch of a new company called Jefferson-North Wing Co., which was created to sell wings to be processed, frozen and distributed by Henry Colt Enterprises in New Jersey. The wings were supposed to be sold in stores by August that year. Dominic was a self-proclaimed "ham" and was a guest on national shows, such as the *Regis Philbin* and the *Today Show*, but he passed away on March 23, 1991, leaving the restaurant in the hands of its manager, Ivano Toscano. That was when the real marketing blitzes began.

Buffalo Wings fiftieth-anniversary T-shirt. *From the author's collection.*

Today, the Anchor Bar is still located at 1047 Main Street, eighty years after it first moved to that location. It has expanded operations to other locations in the Buffalo area, including in the terminal at the Buffalo–Niagara International Airport. It also has locations in the nearby Canadian cities of Hamilton and Burlington, Ontario. And

Exterior view of the Anchor Bar. *From the author's collection.*

wings themselves are now served at nearly every bar and Italian restaurant in the United States, including at local chains, like Duff's, and national chains, like Buffalo Wild Wings, Dominos, Pizza Hut and the like. The city of Buffalo hosts an annual Wing Fest each Labor Day that has attracted nearly one million people since it started in 2001; visitors have consumed more than four million wings at this event. The Anchor Bar won in a "throw down" with Bobby Flay, and the humble wing even won a James Beard Award in 2003 for its "timeless appeal, beloved for quality food that reflects history, character of the community."

Although many versions of Buffalo wings use other hot sauces as a base, the Anchor Bar still uses Frank's Red Hot Sauce, which was first conceived in 1918 and began being bottled in 1920. Wings have become the go-to appetizer for sports games, and according to the National Chicken Council, Americans have consumed more than one billion pounds of wings during each Super Bowl for the last ten years.

Over the forty years' worth of advertisements reviewed for this section, the spelling of Teressa's name changed frequently, although it was most commonly spelled Theresa, not Teressa, which seemed to be preferred starting in the 1980s. The long, humorous, 1969 profile of the Bellissimos' fiftieth anniversary, which was noted a few times above, spelled her name as Theresa, and on her grave, her name is listed as Teresa. But regardless of the spelling of her name—or which version of the Buffalo wing origin story you prefer—Frank and Teressa's Anchor Bar elevated humble chicken wings to great heights. In classic Buffalo innovation style, chicken wings, once discarded or used in stock, are now the most expensive cut of chicken per pound, nearly four times more expensive than legs and thighs, and they are usually more expensive than breast meat as well. And that is certainly a testament to the popularity of Buffalo wings.

CONCLUSION

The Buffalo area in western New York has so much more history than most residents realize, and it has more going for it than national weather reports of snowfall. The pioneers profiled in this book had a profound effect on not just the city or the country but on the world we live in today. If you eat any food made from grain, consider how difficult it was to pick, ship and process grain in the 1840s. The ability to ship grain from the Midwest to the East in days rather than weeks improved more than just the lives of the people in the grain and transportation businesses.

If you had lived in one of the growing urban areas in the 1850s and 1860s, how comfortable would you have been thinking that your only defenses against fire were leather water buckets? Fire engines, fire hydrants and district steam heat meant that people no longer needed to heat their homes with open-hearth fires, the number one cause of most fires of the era. And even when fires did start, people had more reliable and quicker ways to squelch them.

More than 50 percent of the modern workforce is female. Can any of us imagine how difficult it must have been to go to work and have to leave children home alone, out wandering the streets—or worse yet—tied to furniture and locked in a house? Today, daycares provide safe, healthy and educational activities for our children.

Whether or not you believe in capital punishment, electrocution was a much more humane way of carrying out death sentences than the guillotine, firing squads and public hangings. Research conducted on the levels of electricity bodies could tolerate also made electrical generation plants and electric transmission safer.

If you are female and work in any field that was considered appropriate only for males in the mid-1800s, you can thank female doctors, lawyers and architects for blazing the trail for you nearly 150 years ago. And anyone living in hot, arid areas can only survive there because of air conditioning. And even those living in northern climates regularly need cooling comfort in the summer when temperatures reach the nineties or higher.

Can you imagine driving in snow, sleet or heavy rain without windshield wipers? If your wipers have ever failed on you or frozen over, you can understand what drivers in the early 1900s went through. If you are lactose intolerant or just prefer not to use dairy products, you still have plenty of healthy food options today because of the development of soy products as dairy alternatives.

Hopefully, you will not have heart ailments, but if you or a close friend or relative does develop heart problems, can you imagine being forced to use a pacemaker that would keep you in bed for the rest of your life? Implantable pacemakers with replaceable batteries not only save lives but also allow patients the freedom to do virtually whatever they want.

Last, what would the Super Bowl or other major sporting events be like without the ubiquitous Buffalo wing?

Had this been a book just on inventions, several of these pioneers would not have been included; yet their contributions are as important, if not more so, then the actual inventions mentioned within. They all had a profound impact on the city of Buffalo, on the businesses conducted here and on business conducted nationally and around the world. They were true pioneers.

BIBLIOGRAPHY

Barbasch, Adriana. *A Tribute to the First Professional Woman Architect Admitted to the American Institute of Architecture: Louise Bethune, FAIA*. Buffalo, NY: American Institute of Architects, Buffalo/Western New York Chapter, 2006.

Baxter, Henry. *Grain Elevators*. Vol. 26. Buffalo, NY: Buffalo and Erie County Historical Society, 1980.

Dart, Joseph. *The Grain Elevators of Buffalo. Read Before the Society March 13, 1865*. Buffalo, NY: Buffalo and Erie County Historical Society, 1879.

Eberle, S., and J.A. Grande. *Second Looks: A Pictorial History of Buffalo and Erie County*. Norfolk, VA: Donning Company, 1987.

Frederickson, Madelynn P. *The Life and Times of Birdsill Holly*. Lockport, NY: KAX Solutions and Services, 2012.

Greatbatch, Wilson. *Implantable Active Devices: A Commemoration of 25 Years of Pacing*. Clarence, NY: Greatbatch Enterprises Inc., 1983.

———. *The Making of the Pacemaker: Celebrating a Lifesaving Invention*. Amherst, NY: Prometheus Books, 2000.

BIBLIOGRAPHY

Hatch, Alden. *Glenn Curtiss: Pioneer of Aviation*. Guilford, CT: Lyons Press, 2007.

Hays, Johanna. *Louise Blanchard Bethune: America's First Female Professional Architect*. Jefferson, NC: McFarland, 2014.

Ingels, Margaret. *Willis Haviland Carrier, Father of Air Conditioning*. Louisville, KY: Fetter Print Co., 1991.

Little, Karen Berner. *Maria M. Love: The Life and Legacy of a Social Work Pioneer*. Cheektowaga: Western New York Heritage Press, 2003.

Maher-Keplinger, L. *Grain Elevators*. New York: Princeton Architectural Press, 1993.

Mingus, Nancy Blumenstalk. *Buffalo Good Neighbors, Great Architecture*. Charleston, SC: Arcadia Publishing, 2003.

Mitchell, Charles R., and Kirk W. House. *Glenn H. Curtiss, Aviation Pioneer*. Charleston, SC: Arcadia Publishing, 2001.

Osborn, Alex F. *Applied Imagination; Principles and Procedures of Creative Thinking, by Alex. F. Osborn*. New York: Scribner, 1957.

———. *What's Right About Buffalo*. Reprint, Buffalo, NY: Erie Electric Co., 1952.

Osborn, John R. *What's Right About Buffalo*. Buffalo, NY: N.p., 1980.

Rockwell, Mary Rech. *John R. Oishei: Buffalo Businessman and Benefactor*. Buffalo, NY: John R. Oishei Foundation, 2004.

Roseberry, Cecil R. *Glenn Curtiss, Pioneer of Flight*. Syracuse, NY: Syracuse University Press, 1991.

Schultz, E.B. *Weathermakers to the World: The Story of a Company. The Standard of an Industry*. Syracuse, NY: Carrier Engineering Corp., 2012.

Toscani, Ivano. *The Story of Frank and Teressa's Anchor Bar, Home of the Original Buffalo Chicken Wings*. Buffalo, NY: Gallagher Printing Inc., 2003.

Whitford, Noble E. *History of the Canal System of the State of New-York, Together with Brief Histories of the Canals of the United States and Canada.* Albany, NY: Brandow, 1906.

ABOUT THE AUTHOR

This is Nancy Blumenstalk Mingus's fifth book. Her other books include *Teach Yourself Project Management in 24 Hours*; *Buffalo: Good Neighbors, Great Architecture*; *MS-Publisher for Visual Learners*; and *Homes in the US, 1821 to 1860*. She has also written more than sixty articles in magazines such as *Buffalo Spree*, *Computerworld*, *TRAINING*, *Creative Computing* and *Today's Parts Manager*.

In addition to being a freelance writer, Mingus is the president of Mingus Associates Inc., a project management, technology training and consulting company she founded in 1989. She was also a college faculty member at several colleges before retiring from those positions in 2018; she taught at the University of Phoenix for sixteen years and Empire State College for fifteen years, as well as at Columbia University, DeVry University, Pace University, Millard Fillmore College, SUNY at Buffalo and Alfred University. She was also a founding member of the New York State Barn Coalition, the Buffalo chapter of the Project Management Institute and the Downtown Buffalo chapter of Toastmasters International.

Mingus has a master's degree in math education, a master's degree in historic preservation and has completed all her coursework for a PhD in American studies. Her company owns a Gothic Revival house in Knowlesville, New York, which is being painstakingly restored and is now used as the company's corporate office. Mingus resides with her husband on a one-hundred-acre farm in Lyndonville, New York.